BAD
MAN

GULSHAN GROVER

with ROSHMILA BHATTACHARYA

BAD MAN

AN AUTOBIOGRAPHY

Foreword by MAHESH BHATT

EBURY
PRESS

An imprint of Penguin Random House

EBURY PRESS

USA | Canada | UK | Ireland | Australia
New Zealand | India | South Africa | China

Ebury Press is part of the Penguin Random House group of companies
whose addresses can be found at global.penguinrandomhouse.com

Published by Penguin Random House India Pvt. Ltd
7th Floor, Infinity Tower C, DLF Cyber City,
Gurgaon 122 002, Haryana, India

First published in Ebury Press by Penguin Random House India 2019

Copyright: © Gulshan Grover and Roshmila Bhattacharya 2019

ISBN 9780670092062

Typeset in Adobe Garamond Pro by Manipal Digital Systems, Manipal
Printed at Thomson Press India Ltd, New Delhi

www.penguin.co.in

TO MY SON, SANJAY, MY CHILD, MY WORLD, AND SOMEONE WHO HAS ALWAYS MADE ME SO PROUD

CONTENTS

FOREWORD

MAHESH BHATT

It is Ravan and not Ram who makes the Ramayana *so very exciting.*

It was way back in my childhood, in the dark hush of a cinema hall, that I first heard these words of wisdom. I woke up to their full implication much later. My mother pronounced this ageless truth as we sat crunching wafers, enthralled, watching Ravan, played by B.M. Vyas, the top villain of those times in the film *Sampoorna Ramayan*.

Heroes are heroic, but aren't they so very predictable? They save the world and win hearts with their noble deeds. You always know they will triumph in the end. But it's the villain who brings conflict into your story.

'Your hero is not the most important character in your movie, your villain is. Stop swooning over your hero's character and his love interest. Give your heart to crafting a great villain, because, like the cliché goes, behind every successful film is a great bad man,' said the writer Salim Khan to me once.

The Bad Man whose life we are going to get a front-row view of in this book is a Good Man.

Gulshan Grover began his career performing in the Ramlila in humble surroundings on the outskirts of Delhi. He was just five years old, when, using his mother's chunni as a costume, he played the part of a monkey in Hanuman-ji's force, and for which he got a glass of milk and bananas to eat as salary! His performance was so good he progressed slowly to bigger and better roles, and look where he has reached today!

Gulshan has done close to five hundred films out of which thirty-one are international films. Apart from doing British, Canadian, French, German and Italian films, he also has the rare distinction of being the first Indian actor to act in a Polish, Malaysian and Iranian film.

The ability to deconstruct and reinvent one's persona is the lifeblood of all successful durable entertainers all through history. The reason Gulshan Grover has been able to survive in this novelty-seeking business, where the audience is continuously asking for a new, fresh experience, is because he manages to do just that. Gulshan is a shapeshifter. He's like a snake. A snake, because of its ability to shed its old skin and grow a new one, is seen as a symbol of rejuvenation and everlasting youth. In Hinduism, Shiva worship and the worship of a snake go hand in hand.

'Call him Chhappan Tikli,' said Gopal Anna, the reformed gangster who had made a foray into the world of movies as an actor with my musical hit *Sir*. He was referring to Gulshan who had just walked out of the make-up room with his stunning 'get-up' and a face full of pockmarks. Something told me that if Gulshan had succeeded in invoking this response from a real-life gangster-turned-actor, his character would certainly work with the people of this country. And boy, was I right!

'I realized way back in time, Bhatt saab, when I joined the movies, that there was nothing strikingly different about my body to make me stand out. I didn't have the voice of an Amrish Puri or the charisma of a Pran saab to make an instant impact on our impatient, unforgiving audience. So I needed to work a hundred times harder on every role no matter how small or large it was. Once you brutally confront your limitations, they cease to be limitations. They become your assets. My ordinariness was the fuel that kept me hungry for more. That, in short, is my mantra of what you call success.'

But Gulshan is no self-effacing saint. He knows that in show business one must use every trick in the book to stay relevant. In this changing, shifting time, where the consumer gobbles up entertainment by the hour and then spits it out on the pavement, it is getting more and more difficult to stay afloat. For an actor who began his journey from such humble beginnings, it wouldn't be an exaggeration for me to conclude that his life is nothing short of a triumph.

So what has he done in particular to achieve this stunning position? Here's the secret . . .

It was at 5.30 a.m. when my phone pinged one day. 'Just finished reading the script of *Sadak 2*, sir. Loved it. Thank you for making me a part of this journey. Lots of love . . . Gulshan.'

The message made me smile to myself. It was barely ten hours since I had handed the script to him. The very fact that he had ploughed through it and responded with such passion so quickly told me what the enduring icons of the entertainment business have been saying since the dawn of time. Enthusiasm . . . enthusiasm . . . unbridled enthusiasm . . . that's what it's all about.

No wonder that whenever I meet him, the very first thing I say to him is 'Gulshan Grover never over!'

1

THE PRINCE AND THE COMMON MAN

Oslo, Norway

I was being felicitated for my contribution to global cinema at the Norway Film Festival by the Norwegian prime minister, Erna Solberg. When we were on stage, the premier joked that she had thought she would be scared by Bollywood's 'Bad Man'—a badge which I had earned for my role in Subhash Ghai's *Ram Lakhan*—but having seen a few 'bad men' of her own in politics, she didn't find me all that intimidating, rather she found me 'dashing'. As the assembled gathering, which included the mayors of Lørenskog and Skedsmo, Age Tovan and Ole Jacob Flaten, and several ministers and dignitaries, broke into appreciative laughter, the prime minister enunciated in carefully coached Hindi, '*Picture abhi baaki hai*' (The film isn't over yet).

Her words rang true as the first call came through while I was still in the auditorium. It was from the BBC, who wanted to know if I had been invited to dinner by Prince Charles. The invitation had arrived that very morning. I had intimated His Royal Highness, whom I admire, through a mail that I was in the neighbouring Scandinavian country, and in response, he had invited me to fly down and dine with him at his newly acquired Dumfries House in Scotland. I had immediately accepted the offer. When the news leaked out, the British tabloids whipped up a frenzy of headlines about H.R.H. (as the Prince of Wales is fondly called) throwing open the doors of his home to the Bollywood superstar while apparently ditching Her Majesty Queen Elizabeth II on her big day.

On 9 September 2015 at 5.30 p.m. GMT, the eighty-nine-year-old matriarch would be clocking in 23,226 days, sixteen hours, and thirty minutes to enter the record books as the world's longest-ruling monarch, surpassing even the reign of her great-great-grandmother Queen Victoria. Her Majesty was to officially open the Scottish Borders Railway on the day to mark this achievement. There were speculations in the press that the heir to the crown was deliberately skipping the occasion to host the 'spectacularly rich' Gulshan Grover who had 400-plus films to his credit. I confirmed to the BBC that I would, indeed, be dining with Prince Charles. However, I wasn't sure about the description—'spectacularly rich'—appended to my name. 'Show me the money?' I had laughed, and unperturbed by the media buzz, I arrived at H.R.H.'s Scottish mansion the following afternoon. There are times when it felt almost surreal that a boy who grew up in the middle of nowhere would be brushing shoulders with royalty . . .

I had first met Prince Charles over a decade ago. The meeting was set up by my friend and his personal physician, Dr Mosaraf Ali, who had put my second wife, Kashish, back on her feet after an accident. A quick word about Kashish who is beautiful, both inside and outside. I know she wouldn't like me to talk about her so I will only say I remain grateful to this wonderful lady for having touched my life. Much respect. Getting back to Muzu bhai, as Dr Ali is called by his friends, he had fixed a ten-minute interaction with H.R.H. at Highgrove House in Gloucestershire—Prince Charles's home since 1980. His sons, Prince William and Prince Harry, also spent much of their early childhood at Highgrove

House and it had a lived-in feel. I noticed carelessly kicked-off sneakers—obviously belonging to the young princes—lying around, reminding me of my son, Sanjay.

The thirty-seven-acre estate was also used for organic farming, and to my delight, I saw buffaloes ambling around sedately, with more cattle grazing in the fields beyond. Having started my life in similar, though far more modest, surroundings, it was as though I was in the home of a familiar friend rather than a British royal.

Of course, Tri-Nagar, where I grew up, while less than an hour's bus drive from Delhi's bustling centre and its historic landmarks like the Rashtrapati Bhavan, was a world apart, miles away from civilization. Kachcha dirt roads led one to either the bus stop, which was ten to twelve kilometres away, or the railway tracks. I belonged to a family that lived on the fringes of India's capital city, dotted with the pucca brick houses of the owners of large farms along with the shanties of the very poor, which had illegally come up on the farmland. For someone who at one point of time went without a meal for days, it was unbelievable to be dining with the Prince of England. Such things happened only in fairy tales . . . or in the movies.

Muzu bhai was slightly peeved because despite him having underlined the dress code, I had turned up wearing an informal turtleneck with a suit rather than the mandatory tie. I pointed out to him that the invitation had taken me by surprise, and I wasn't carrying a tie. Our host, who was dressed in a stylish suit and tie, however, didn't seem perturbed by my choice of attire. When we got talking, I found H.R.H. to be a warm and wonderful man who cared deeply for humanity and wanted to give back to society some of what he had received as his birthright.

Suddenly, taking everyone by surprise, H.R.H. decided to give me a tour of the Highgrove Royal Gardens himself, with Muzu bhai and his entourage, which included his assistants Catie Bland and Siobhan Bucknall, for company. While we were strolling, the Prince referred to his 'shop' a few times, so, curious, I asked about it. He told me it was located right there on the estate, but because it was a Saturday, it was shut. He had it specially opened for me and I discovered to my surprise that it sold everything, from dressing gowns to coasters and candles. It also stocked cherry wine, orange marmalade and strawberry preserve—all the produce organically produced on the estate. I bought ten sets of candles knowing that every penny from the sale would go towards a noble cause.

Back home, our locality had no electricity till six miles away and as soon as the sun went down, it would get pitch dark. The last stretch to our home was through paddy fields. I would walk through them with the fear of snakes and small wild animals dogging my footsteps. There were no welcoming lights at home either, but it was lit up by the camaraderie of my six siblings—my elder brother and sister Ramesh Chandra and Raj didi, along with my younger sisters Urmila, Rita, Ramana and Akanksha. We had studied together in the light of lanterns and candles. Almost a quarter of a century later, I bought some candles from the Prince's shop and imagined the proud smiles on the faces of my parents, Pitaji Bishamber Nath Grover and Mai Ramrakhi, when I handed them over.

Prince Charles was eventually called away to keep another commitment, a visitor he had kept waiting. As he was walking away, H.R.H. suddenly turned and asked, 'Hey, Gulshan, how can I get in touch with you?' That query took everyone by surprise, including me. Being a star and a familiar name, I had never had visiting cards printed. Fortunately, I did have a press kit I usually handed out to Hollywood executives during my frequent trips to Los Angeles. Along with some of my interviews and work-related information, it also had some personal details like my address and phone number. I had one with me that I handed over to the Prince.

I wasn't expecting him to remember me or even to meet him again, but we did, on 24 October 2005, at Clarence House in London's St James Palace. To my surprise, I was received as his personal guest and seated in H.R.H.'s personal study. I noticed several half-read books lying around the room, their covers down, revealing his varied reading interests. I had started my education in a small government school in our locality, but I had always loved books and they had helped me develop a command over not just Hindi and Urdu but English as well, even though angrezi was an alien language in my environment then. I smiled as I meandered along, till the butler came to enquire if he could get me something. I asked for a cup of tea, he returned saying H.R.H. was wondering if I wouldn't like something stronger since it was such a cold day. I laughed and told him I would stick to my cuppa.

A little later, I was ushered upstairs. As I ascended the last stair, I found H.R.H. waiting for me in the hallway. 'Look at you, looking marvellous, getting younger every day!' he exclaimed, leading me down the corridor and into his private chamber. Once again, our meeting extended well beyond its allotted time. H.R.H. was flying out the same evening and by the time he came down with his head of business development, Oliver Brind, and me, his team looked distinctly frazzled. In the winter, the sun sets early in the United Kingdom and the team was worried that the chopper carrying the Prince and his entourage might not be able to take off if it got too dark. H.R.H. introduced me to them, saying, 'This is Gulshan Grover, the famous actor from India.' That morning, the *Daily Mirror* had carried an article referring to me as 'Bollywood's Bond Villain'. The Prince's cousin recognized me from that piece and asked curiously, 'Are you really doing a Bond film?'

It seemed that Her Majesty's Secret Service evoked much interest even among the British royal family and so I confirmed that I would be doing *Casino Royale*, the twenty-first film in the popular Bond franchise. I said that I would be playing the much-coveted role of the main antagonist, Le Chiffre, a chess whiz banker and mathematical genius who services many of the world's top terrorists and eventually takes on Bond, played by Daniel Craig. It's another story that the news was leaked out prematurely by a local reporter-friend I had confided in about the casting coup, a week before the formal announcement was made, and the upset producers subsequently replaced me with Mads Mikkelsen.

The Prince and I met a few more times, including once at a dinner in Mumbai, before I flew to visit him in Scotland. I was picked up by his car from the airport and driven to the in-house estate hotel. A jeep with escorts was waiting for me there and I was whisked away for a guided tour of the premises. The invitation had urged me to arrive before sunset so I could see the estate in the daylight.

Like at Highgrove House, I was given the tour of Dumfries House too. And as always, I found myself flashbacking to my humble beginning when we had lived in a little brick house with wooden slats for the roof, eventually replaced with the slates used to line pavements. My father was a self-taught scholar who read a lot and struggled daily to make ends meet. I was a bright student, but I may never have graduated high school and continued my education in one of Delhi's prestigious colleges had it not been for the benevolence of strangers.

Life had been tough then, but there were never any complaints because what we lacked in material possessions was made up by the wisdom of my parents and the warmth of my siblings. It didn't matter if I didn't have a separate bedroom, a study table with a lamp or a wardrobe full of designer wear. That was my home, just as this was home for the Prince.

After freshening up, I was taken to meet my host. He greeted me graciously, dressed in the traditional Scottish kilt. While I was leaving the dining table, H.R.H. asked me how I liked Dumfries House. I blurted out that it would make for a picture-postcard setting for a film, especially the front steps. His cousin shook his head at me reprovingly, saying firmly, 'No shooting here.' But the Prince smiled. 'For you, Gulshan, it's okay.'

I have come a long way since those days, but the memories come flooding back, particularly on momentous occasions like when I was on stage with the prime minister of Norway or hobnobbing with Hollywood A-listers or dining with the Prince of Wales. Or now, shooting for my 500th Bollywood film, *Sooryavanshi* (with Rohit Shetty and Akshay Kumar) and working on *Sadak 2* with Alia and Mahesh Bhatt. Some may have described these moments as a dream come true, but growing up, I didn't even have the luxury to dream.

When you are consumed with hunger, when you are struggling to survive, you don't dare dream. You just hope that you can carry the battle forward to another day. And that's exactly what I did.

2

ALL THE WORLD'S A STAGE

My earliest memory as a toddler is going to the nearby government school with my mother holding my little hand tightly in hers. Even after I went into my classroom, Chaiji as I call her, refused to leave, standing by the school wall, her eyes fixed on me as I studied or skipped around the playground, constantly reassuring herself that I wasn't miserable or had fallen and hurt myself. After a few weeks, her presence by the wall was noted and she was firmly told by the teachers that she couldn't stand there and keep vigil. My mother, otherwise a gentle and amiable person, could not be persuaded to stay away in this instance. Moved by her tears, the owner of a small shop located opposite the school, which stocked up on biscuits and sweets that the children would run out for when school was over for the day, allowed her to sit outside it. She would patiently wait there for the last bell to ring so she could take me home with her.

Pitaji was a Hindu scholar while Chaiji was a devout Sikh who always carried the pocket-sized Gutka, which had chosen vaanis (verses or songs) from the Guru Granth Sahib and which she would read and recite while she waited for me. Occasionally, she would stroll up to the wall and steal a glance at me from over it to make sure I was fine. It was a few years before my doting mother could be convinced to let me be left alone at school.

My father was an enlightened man who refused to be cowed down by the circumstances of his birth. He compensated for the lack of amenities with pearls of wisdom that he imparted to my siblings and me. As a result, even though we had no electricity at home and grew up in darkness, I was never depressed. Pitaji would constantly assure us that our condition would improve one day soon and that the daily struggle was but a passing phase.

'Focus on your studies, that is your ladder to a better life,' he would reiterate. With these words constantly ringing in my ears, I never entered a classroom without my homework done. And unlike many of my classmates, I was never reprimanded by my teachers because my mind was miles away from the lesson being taught. My uniform was never stained with mud from the rowdy fights in the playground and my grades always made Pitaji proud. I would go with Chaiji to the gurudwara every morning and during festivals, participate in kar seva, which included sweeping the floor and washing the langar dishes. I would respectfully touch the feet of the elders I met there and seek their blessings. They would return home and pull up their own children for not being like Gulshan. For my friends I was a paragon of virtue and, so, a bloody nuisance. It's ironical that this 'good boy' went on to make a career playing the 'bad man' even though I am nothing like the characters I breathe life into.

The sanskar (values) that was a part of my upbringing came to good use when I was in the ninth standard. Our financial situation had deteriorated further by then and both my brother, Ramesh bhai, and I were required to work to supplement the family income. Since I had afternoon school, the mornings were free and I would set out from home early with my school bag, freshly laundered uniform and some rotis tied in an old cloth. I also lugged along samples of detergents and disinfectants with an order book. I would visit the affluent neighbourhoods close by,

like Punjabi Bagh, hoping to convince the ladies who lived in the
kothis there to buy their household supplies from me.

Since the stuff I was peddling was not branded, it was not easy
persuading them to buy from me. I think it was the sincerity they
saw in my eyes, along with my courteous manners, that eventually
won them over. Or perhaps they noticed my school uniform and
the rotis in the same bag as the samples and were moved by my
plight. Whatever the reasons, despite their initial misgivings,
these ladies started placing orders with me every week. Ramesh
bhai would deliver the supplies—be it detergents for washing
clothes or disinfectants for the toilet—to them the next day. To
my parents' delight, I soon built up a large and loyal clientele
who would always order from me, sometimes despite not having
finished earlier supplies. They even gave away stuff to their help
so they would not have to turn me away from their door empty-
handed.

These ladies were very sympathetic towards me. Some of
them had seen me sitting at a roadside tea stall, eating the rotis
my mother packed for my lunch every morning. I couldn't carry
a curry along because I was afraid that the gravy might leak and
stain my school uniform. After learning that I headed for school
directly after finishing my rounds, some of these wonderful ladies
even let me change into my uniform in the privacy of their homes.
I still remember them with gratitude because it is only thanks to
them that I was able to continue going to school. I passed high
school with distinction in five subjects. My two friends, Dinesh
Jain and Pradeep Sharma, and I were the first students from our
small government school to get a first class. We were the *medhavi
chhatras*, students par excellence, and our names were painted on
the blackboard outside the principal's office and there they have
remained for posterity.

In our school, English was taught in Hindi. The teachers
would read aloud sentences in *angrezi*, and then translate them

into Hindi for us. Even Charles Dickens's famous novel, *Oliver Twist*, was taught to us in Hinglish. I found the process tedious and exasperating, and eventually taught myself English so I could read the books myself. Thanks to our high grades and fluency in English, in 1971, after passing out of school, Dinesh and I got admission to Shri Ram College of Commerce (SRCC), one of the oldest and most prestigious educational institutes in Delhi.

I had to walk nine kilometres through kachcha, mud-splattered lanes to the nearest bus stop. After that I had to change three buses to get to college, which was in North Campus of the Delhi University. There was a short-cut that would have saved me precious time, but it meant crossing the railway tracks. I also had to jump over wood planks with yawning gaps—a makeshift bridge of sorts over a gushing river—and ran the risk of falling in and being washed away. With these dangers looming large on her mind, my mother made me solemnly promise that I would always take the longer route, and I kept my word. But while it wasn't all that difficult to turn away from the enticing aroma of freshly fried samosas and bread pakoras wafting in from the college canteen because I had no money to spare, for the first time in my life I would wake up every morning wishing we lived closer to the university so I didn't have to begin my day three hours before my classmates.

The cut-offs required to get into SRCC were far higher than those for other colleges affiliated to Delhi University, with the result that it drew the brightest minds. Arjan Kumar Sikri, with whom I shared my desk in class, topped every exam he appeared for and was lauded for his writing skills. He served as judge and acting chief justice of the Delhi High Court. He was also chief justice of the Punjab and Haryana High Court and was sworn in as a Supreme Court judge in 2013. He was voted among the fifty most influential people in intellectual property in the world in a survey conducted by the Managing Intellectual Property Association (MIPA) in

2007 and delivered many landmark judgments, including one on the validity of the authentication of Aadhar. We stayed in touch even after graduating from college and remain good friends. In fact, I have met him at his home in Delhi at regular intervals and we have a blast catching up on old times.

Senior advocate and till recently the Union Finance Minister and Minister of Corporate Affairs in the Indian cabinet, Arun Jaitley, was also my batchmate. Arun was the president of the students' union whose joint secretary, Vijay Goel, is another big name today in Indian politics, currently serving as Minister of State for Parliamentary Affairs and Statistic and Implementation in the NDA government. During his stint as Minister of State for Youth Affairs and Sports, Vijay launched the National Talent Search Portal which connects talented sportspersons to the Sports Authority of India for training and guidance. He has been a dear and dependable friend since my college days. And I had the privilege of watching Arun spar in fluent English with top-ranking students during inter-collegiate debates. He cut a dashing figure in his trendy T-shirts and was among the ten most handsome guys in college during our time, with an IQ to match his style quotient. Arun's partner in these debates was usually another friend, Rakesh Mathur, who is now the president of many hotel chains. Together, they won many trophies for our college.

My friend Sunil Sethi, who was known for his flamboyance, had seen more of the world than many of us. He is a style icon who has taken Indian fashion to unimaginable global heights and is now the president of the Fashion Design Council of India. Rajat Sharma and I were also very close, but he was poles apart from Sunil. Back then, Rajat liked to dress in a simple kurta and pyjama or trousers. With his razor-sharp intelligence and an innate inquisitiveness about the world around him, which expressed itself through endless queries and fearless opinions, Rajat went on to become the chairman and editor-in-chief of India TV. He became a household name with his TV show, *Aap Ki Adalat*, the longest-running show on Indian television. I have been invited to Rajat's courtroom many times and grilled mercilessly, without being shown any consideration of being a college buddy. Jokes apart, Rajat is one friend I know I can always turn to in a crisis. Ritu bhabhi and he are just a call away. In fact, even Shah Rukh Khan admitted to me once that he had told his kids that if they were ever in trouble they should dial Rajat uncle and he would help them. I told Shah Rukh that this was exactly what I had said to my son Sanjay. Since then we have a friendly ongoing banter on who said this first about the man-for-all-seasons, the ever-dependable Rajat Sharma.

Also among my college mates and friends are Atul Gupta, the head of the Osho meditation centres, and Raman Lamba of Tata; Deepak Khetrapal, managing director and CEO, Orient Cement; and Rayan Karanjawala, managing partner of Karanjawala & Co., who has a law degree to boot and is one of Delhi's movers and shakers who has always been by my side.

Back then, SRCC was the college for studious students who rarely left the classroom or the library. Since many of us were not from privileged backgrounds, we would stand outside the library for hours, waiting for a student to vacate one of the sixty chairs inside so that we could browse through some of the books we couldn't afford to buy. But unlike some of the other students, I didn't just roost in the college library. I also made an impression on the stage, my histrionics bringing the college laurels.

Sunil Sethi and I acted in many plays together, with him playing my son in one of them, as part of SRCC's Fine Arts Society. I was voted president and also the secretary of the Fine Arts Society. In fact, I soon became so popular as an actor that I was invited by the students of Indraprastha College and Miranda House—the all-girls college opposite ours—to play the male roles in their plays much to the envy of the other boys. Along with my batchmates, we changed the impression that SRCC students only saw the world myopically through thick, black-rimmed glasses. For me, to borrow a quote from the Bard, 'All the world's a stage, and all the men and women merely players.' And it was on this stage that I found my identity and, later, my vocation.

From amateur college plays, I went on to dabble in professional theatre. My ever-supportive parents had saved for months to buy me an old Lambretta scooter. I would ride it to the Little Theatre Group Auditorium in Delhi's Connaught Place, hoping to land a part in one of the plays. The bigger roles would be gobbled up by senior actors like Gemini Kumar, Brij Bhushan Sahni, Uttara Baokar, Meenakshi Thakur, Naresh Suri and Veena Goad, to name a few. But once in a while, I would get lucky and bag a small role that gave me the opportunity to rub shoulders with these professionals, watch their performances from the wings and learn from them up close. I also interacted with actors of the National School of Drama (NSD) which was located right next door. Shankar Market, one of the oldest markets in the capital, was always buzzing with creative talent. I would go there often to soak in the arts even though I was studying commerce.

Surprisingly for an actor, I didn't grow up with much exposure to cinema. There were no movie theatres in our neighbourhood and even if there had been, I had no money to buy tickets. There was a tin shed, across from the railway tracks, towards Indralok, five to six kilometres from my place, inside which movies were screened. During summer holidays, all the kids would line up outside this makeshift theatre, silent as mice, our ears perked to catch the dialogue as a movie played inside. Some brats had drilled a hole in one of the tin sheets and we would take turns to peek through it and catch the action on the screen. However, even with our eyes focused on the film, we would keep an eye out for the watchman. If he spotted any of us during his rounds, he would not hesitate to give us a sound thrashing. Sometimes the lathi would be hurled from a distance, catching us unawares. After this happened a couple of times, we took turns to catch the film and watch out for the guard. All this made movie-viewing a unique and unforgettable experience.

I couldn't have seen more than ten or twenty films during my entire childhood. I watched some of them when the travelling cinema stopped by our locality. There was great excitement as the projector was cranked. We would sit cross-legged on the open ground in anticipation of what would play out on the white screen that was hung out in front. I don't remember the titles of the films I watched, but I do remember that one of them featured Dharmendra-ji. Later, I watched a few of Manoj Kumar saab and Dev Anand saab's films at cinema halls close to my college. One of them was the iconic *Guide* with Dev saab as Raju Guide romancing Waheeda Rehman-ji who played the dancer Rosie and swayed to the tunes of '*Aaj phir jeene ki tamanna hai, aaj phir marna ka irada hai*'. These films transported me to a magical technicolour world, far removed from my own often starkly dark one. They took me on an adventure of song and dance, drama and melodrama. They turned acting into a passion.

My interest in acting was sparked off at an early age because of the Ramlila that my father and his friends organized every year, funded by collections and donations from the shops in our locality. A dramatic re-enactment of Lord Rama's life, inspired by Tulsidas's *Ramayan* and the *Ramcharitmanas*, it played out on a makeshift stage during the annual festival of Dussehra. The festival ended with an effigy of Ravan, the demon king who had abducted Sita from the forest, being burnt to mark the triumph of good over evil.

My father was the script and dialogue writer and he took his responsibility very seriously, reading all versions of the Ramayana to enrich his own writing. Since Pitaji could read only Urdu, I was given the task of reading out books in Hindi and English and translating them for him. As a result, I know the Ramayana, along with the *Janamsakhis*, like the back of my hand. The *Janamsakhis* are considered to be the biographies of the first Sikh guru, Shri Guru Nanak Devji. Chaiji would read out stories from them every night.

During the Ramlila, my sisters, Ramesh bhai and I were allowed to stay up way past our usual bedtime. I would sit mesmerized as the story I had read out to my father was enacted before my eyes. While the elders played the main parts, some of us kids landed smaller roles. The naughty ones went into Ravan's army, while angels like me were picked up for Hanuman's vanar sena. One year, I remember sitting atop a tree on stage, eating a banana, naked except for my mother's dupatta tied like a loincloth to protect my modesty. My first induction into the monkey army was around the age of five, and from that experience was born a lifelong love for dramatics.

The elders, including my father, in the Ramlila committee were very particular that the actors should 'live' their characters in real life too. So, when Ram was living in a palace in Ayodhya, the actor playing him was fed meals befitting a prince by the locals. But as soon as he moved to the forest with Sita and Lakshman, the actors could eat only fruit and berries, and were expected to live rough, sleeping on the floor at home during the period of their fourteen-year exile.

The actor playing Hanuman could also eat only fruit and drink milk. In fact, all the performers, through the duration of the Ramlila, were sternly instructed to give up non-vegetarian food and alcohol. They even vowed not to get intimate with their spouses. Once the curtain came down, they would be sent to take a dip in the Ganga before they returned to their normal lives till the next year and the next Ramlila.

When I began studying acting formally, I realized that what my father and the elders had practised in our village during the

Ramlila is called 'method acting'. It calls for sincere, emotionally expressive performances and is built on a technique developed by the Russian actor–director Konstantin Stanislavsky.

Meanwhile, I graduated from college in 1974 with flying colours and applied for a master's degree in commerce at SRCC while I was seriously contemplating my choice of profession. My college had promised me a job as a professor and the chair of the Fine Arts Society after my post-graduation. My family wanted me to join a bank, pointing out that it was a steady job with a secure future and that it brought in good money. But I surprised my father with a request. I asked to be allowed to go to Mumbai so I could try my luck in films.

Although shocked, Pitaji masked the disappointment he must have felt over my seemingly frivolous decision. He told me that he would give me six months to get the acting bug out of my system. 'If you don't make it in these six months, you will return home to Delhi and pursue a career more suited to your degree without dwelling on the past,' he told me firmly. I agreed and went to Chaiji to tell her that I was going to Mumbai to become an actor. My mother reacted simply, 'Do whatever you want to during the day but come back home every night to sleep.' When I told her that would not be possible because I would be relocating to another city hundreds of miles away, she started to cry.

I understood her emotional need to see me at home every evening; it symbolized her love and protectiveness. This was the same person who had stood outside my school for hours when I was a child, waiting to bring me home. I may have grown up since, but for her, I was still her Gulshan, the child she could not let out of her sight in case I should lose my way or hurt myself. Every time I broached the subject of leaving for Mumbai, my mother would become anxious and fall ill. As a result, my trip was delayed by almost six months, till my brother and sisters finally convinced my mother to let me go and pursue my dream. Chaiji eventually agreed on the condition that I would write her a letter every day. My son, Sanjay, will vouch for the fact that I have kept my word and wrote to his grandmother every single day during those early years in Mumbai.

Then, just when the little bird was getting ready to fly the nest, my mother learnt that Mumbai was close to the sea and once again panicked. Chaiji had grown up in Punjab, in a home very close to the Bhakra Nangal Dam. She remembered the water overflowing and sweeping away homes and lives during the monsoon every year. That had made her paranoid about water. 'It's too dangerous, you can't go to Mumbai,' she stated, fearfully. But finally, against her better judgement, she gave in when I solemnly vowed never to go near the sea.

For five years, till she visited the city and saw for herself that the sea in Mumbai is usually a serene blue and nothing like an angry dam bursting forth, I kept my promise to her. Not even when I was strolling with friends on the road alongside Juhu Beach or even when they ridiculed me for refusing to go into the sea with them, did I break my word to my mother. I did not set foot on the sandy beach till she came to Mumbai and agreed that the sea here is safe to wade in for most of the year. The 'Bad Man' of the movies remained a 'Good Son'. He still is one.

3

AN ACTOR IN PREP

After promising my mother that I would write to her every day and would never go near the sea, I left for the City of Dreams, chasing after my own technicolour dream. I had never visited Mumbai before. For me, the city was just a photograph which I had seen and which I had read about in books. Worried about letting me take off to an unknown place where I knew no one, my anxious parents accompanied me to the home of a friend, Prakash Sharma, who lived in Delhi, half a kilometre or so away. Prakash's elder brother, Subhash, was studying at the Film and Television Institute of India (FTII) in Pune. We had never met, but at the behest of his younger brother, Subhash bhai (whose daughter, Madalsa, is married to Mithun Chakraborty's eldest son Mimoh), agreed to come down to Mumbai during the weekend and take me around.

It was early 1975. Subhash bhai was waiting at Bombay Central Station when I stepped off the train. I had grown up in Delhi and was an SRCC graduate, but before this, I had never travelled anywhere alone. I was an over-protected little boy whose mother never let him out of her sight for more than a few hours. So, on my own, in a new city, I was petrified and perhaps a tad too naïve. Together, Subhash bhai and I explored the neighbourhood. I was delighted by the cluster of movie theatres, from Maratha

Mandir, Minerva and Royal Cinema to Jamuna, Apsara, Naaz and Novelty. Suddenly, the tin shed and travelling cinema of my childhood seemed a lifetime away. This was Mumbai where the dream factory was based, I expected to find the glamorous film stars I had seen onscreen, strolling around or driving down the streets. To my disappointment, I did not spot any of the famous faces I had grown up with in the city of my dreams.

Subhash bhai and I then hopped into a local train which took us to Victoria Terminus, since renamed Chhatrapati Shivaji Maharaj Terminus. After a tour of Marine Drive and what the locals call 'town', we moved towards Bandra, traditionally known as the 'Queen of the Suburbs'. Back then, the city, for most people, ended at Bandra, with the exception of Juhu and its beach. Juhu was where the famous movie stars lived, while Bandra—particularly the legendary Marina Guest House at the junction of Linking Road and S.V. Road—was home to starry-eyed strugglers like me. I got myself a bed in the dormitory there and slept with the reassuring dream that one day soon my name too would light up the marquee.

My new residence was on the main road, within walking distance of Bandra station from where I could catch the local train to anywhere in town and keep an appointment. It was also conveniently located near the National Dhaba, a no-frills eatery whose rajma-chawal, kali dal and alu-mattar were value for money for cash-strapped boys like me. Even better was its owner, a large-hearted Sardarji, who offered a mix of lentils for free. You only had to buy rotis and you would get yourself a wholesome meal for a couple of rupees. The dhaba was my regular hangout for lunches and dinners because that was all I could afford back then. There was an Irani restaurant on the ground floor of Marina Guest House and I would duck into it once in a while for anda-pav, the Irani equivalent of bread and omelette, and chai. For special occasions, which were rare, there was Lucky Restaurant diagonally opposite, famous for its lip-smacking biryani.

It didn't take me very long to befriend the other boarders at Marina Guest House, many of whom had been hanging out there for years, some for even a decade or more, hoping to break into the movies. Aspiring actors, directors, writers and singers left me wide-eyed with the wealth of their experiences, even though many of them remained on the fringes of Bollywood.

A few did make it, among them Ashok Mehta, the cinematographer of Shekhar Kapur's *Bandit Queen,* who bagged the National Award for *36 Chowringhee Lane,* directed by Aparna Sen. In later years, he lit me up beautifully in Subhash Ghai's *Ram Lakhan,* contributing significantly to my 'Bad Man' image. There was also Gogi Anand, first cousin of the Anand brothers—Chetan, Dev and Vijay—who went on to direct films like *Darling Darling* and *Doosri Sita.*

The first floor of the guesthouse was for 'janta class' boarders like me. The second floor was also allotted to the strugglers. On the third floor were the 'permanent' residents like Gogi Anand, Ashok Mehta and writer–director Rajat Rakshit, along with the landladies whose trust they had earned over the years. Inmates like me were locked out of the top floor at night by a wrought-iron grill door at the top of the stairs.

In the crowd of boarders, a gentleman called Manmohan stood out. He had been the editor of a popular Urdu newspaper in Delhi and wrote under the pen name 'Talkh'. He had given up his job and a successful career to come to Mumbai with dreams of writing and directing a film. We soon got chatting and Manmohan bhai was impressed to learn that I had done my master's from SRCC. Back then, there weren't too many educated people in the film industry, and so, wowed by my academic qualifications, he offered to share his room, which had two beds, with me.

I was happy to pay for my bed and move into his room that offered me more privacy than the noisy dorm I had shared with five or six others. Manmohan bhai was not a nonentity in this anonymous city. He had come from Delhi armed with congratulatory letters and photographs taken with Bollywood bigwigs from his days as a well-known editor. At the time, these friends had offered to help him should he move to Mumbai, some of the leading actors even promising to work in his film. But later, when he reminded them of their promise, many of them stopped taking his calls. Those he managed to connect with were of little use to him.

By the time we met, Manmohan bhai was disillusioned with the world of art and artifice, and like his pen name 'Talkh', which in Urdu means characterized by sharpness and severity, harsh, bitter, virulent, he vented during our nightly chats. I quickly realized that all the stories I had heard growing up of Dharmendra-ji, one of the contestants of the first *Filmfare* talent hunt contest, who landed from Punjab, caught the eye of film-maker Arjun Hingorani and became an overnight star, were not quite correct. There were years of struggle, sweat and suffering, behind the sparkle of showbiz. Even Dharmendra-ji had returned home, disillusioned, only to be called back by a telegram from Bimal Roy informing him that he would be playing the second lead in *Bandini*, along with Ashok Kumar and Nutan. As a student of commerce, I quickly understood that my approach was all wrong. I wasn't going to catch the eye of a producer who was driving past in his swanky wheels while I stood outside the now-defunct Pamposh restaurant opposite National College in Bandra. I also wasn't going to land a dream debut hanging out at the Mehboob Studio car park waiting for a film-maker to step out of one of the studio floors for a smoke. That was just a pipedream. There were others, many far better looking than me, who had been doing the same thing for years for the ratio to work in my favour.

To add to my troubles, a handsome young actor, the brother-in-law of a much-loved star of yesteryear hits, had borrowed Rs 300 from me and disappeared, leaving me in dire straits. I couldn't ask for more money from my parents knowing that they were already stretching themselves thin. But without it, I couldn't pay the rent. The only way I could dodge the landladies was to sneak into the guesthouse late at night when everyone had gone to bed. But I would get caught when I would have to go up to take a call from home.

Those days there were no cell phones. The only phone extension in our guesthouse was outside the apartment of these ladies on the top floor. The grill door, which locked us out from the fourth floor during the night and early in the morning, was opened once the landladies were up, so we could take our calls standing there on the landing. This gave them an opportunity to collar some of us for a chat and give others like me, who had fallen back on the rent, a tongue-lashing. I'm pretty sure that they were very kind, but because of my pending dues, I would often come down red-faced, with the choicest of abuses ringing in my ears.

Having joined the queue of rejects and dejects, I would often drive down to Pune for a break. I stayed as Subhash bhai's guest in his room in the FTII campus. There, exposure to a formal acting course showed me what I was doing wrong. I must have visited the institute twenty to thirty times, if not more, and during my frequent visits to Pune, I made the acquaintance of actor Mithun Chakraborty, editor–director David Dhawan and writer, producer, director and lyricist Ravindra Peepat. I also met Odia film-maker Manmohan Mahapatra and Manmohan Singh, director of Punjabi films and cinematographer of many of Yash Chopra's films, including *Chandni*, *Dilwale Dulhania Le Jayenge* and *Dil To Pagal Hai*. Shravan Kumar, Harish Kumar, Rahul Senger, Chitrarth, Mala Jaggi, Rakesh Ranjan, Jagmohan, Abha Dhulia and Rameshwari are others I remember from those days. I sat for lectures with Subhash bhai during the day and every evening, after an early dinner, I watched films.

I had always been an avid film buff and I never missed a show when at FTII. The popular international movies played in the big theatres and some in the New Classroom Theatres (CRT). The FTII theatres only screened classics like the German silent horror film, *The Cabinet of Dr. Caligari*, Vittorio De Sica's *Bicycle Thieves* (a masterpiece of Italian neorealism), Jean-Luc Godard's French crime drama *Breathless* and Stanley Kubrick's dystopian crime film, *A Clockwork Orange*. These films were my first exposure to world cinema, and I was entranced.

I also watched some fantastic diploma films made by the students, including S.P. Sinha's (popular as Shatrughan Sinha now) *And Unto the Void* and Mithun-da's *Love Is*. I also remember an abstract film made by Rahul Dasgupta and Uday, aka Dhruv, as also films featuring Jaya Bhaduri, Jalal Agha and Danny Denzongpa. I returned with my mind made up. Pitaji had given me six months in Mumbai to find myself. I packed my bags and returned to Delhi after three months, having lost the battle.

Even though they didn't say much, my parents and siblings must have been really shocked by my appearance. I was skeletal, having cut down on my meals, my sunken eyes reflecting the humiliation I had been through in Mumbai. They reassured me that all was not lost. I had passed the difficult CA exam before I left for Mumbai and there were banks offering me lucrative jobs. My college, too, renewed its offer to hire me as a professor and make me head of SRCC's Dramatics Society. The world was beckoning me, but my heart was still in Mumbai.

I approached my father and told him that I wanted to go back even though the city had treated me so badly, but this time I didn't want to be on a deadline. I needed time and formal training to learn my strengths and weaknesses as an actor. I was aware that training would cost money, big money, but my parents didn't blink. I think Chaiji must have sold off some of her jewellery while Pitaji mortgaged the house where we lived to fund me. And they did this without any fuss or ever telling me.

I left Delhi again, this time for Pune, with plans to enrol at the FTII like Subhash bhai. But my plans immediately hit a roadblock. A month-long agitation lead to the institute discontinuing its acting course. So, I returned to Mumbai, undecided, unsure.

Then, Professor Roshan Taneja, the guru of acting, suddenly decided to open an institute in Mumbai. He was the first and only bona fide acting teacher in the country at the time. I learnt that he was a pioneer in method acting, having trained in New York's Neighbourhood Playhouse School of Theatre under Sydney Pollack, the Oscar-winning director, and Sanford Meisner, the American actor and acting teacher who developed the 'Meisner Technique'. He had returned to India and set up the acting department at FTII in 1963, two years after the institute started. For the next twelve years, right till 1975, he had conducted the two-year course and nurtured brilliant talents like Jaya Bhaduri, Naseeruddin Shah, Shabana Azmi, Om Puri, Shatrughan Sinha, Asrani, Subhash Ghai and Mithun Chakraborty, to name a few.

The Roshan Taneja School of Acting offered a one-year acting course for aspiring actors who wanted to learn the craft under experts and evolve as a person, emerging from the school ready to 'act' truthfully. I joined the school confident that this time around I would be in good hands. Anil Kapoor, Mazhar Khan, Surendra Pal Singh, Madan Jain, Rajhans Singh and Rajesh Mathur were among my classmates. There was also Wasim Khan, aka Vicky, the son of Shashi Kapoor's chauffeur, and Shehzad Askari, actress Mumtaz-ji's brother. We were a batch of around twenty students under the tutelage of Roshan Taneja, whom we all addressed as 'sir'.

His protégés from the institute like Mithun-da, Om Puri saab, Geeta Khanna, Phunsukh Ladakhi and Benjamin Gilani were hired as teachers. We also had visiting faculty like Jaya-ji, Shabana-ji, Shatru-ji and Reeta Bhaduri-ji who would swing by on afternoons when they were not shooting or in the evenings after an early pack-up to conduct workshops. It was thrilling to see these actors I had only seen onscreen so far, up close. Many teachers, like Mithun-da, were struggling actors themselves who were looking for a break. Once we got acquainted, they would hang out with us, sharing their experiences.

One of the lessons we learnt was 'improvisation', the most important exercise for an actor to find his emotional reach and range. We would pick out a situation and inform Professor saab, along with the actor who would partner with us. Sometimes in the evening, after classes, the seniors would put up an 'improvisation' too. I particularly remember one by Reeta-ji, the ever-smiling Bengali actress from Lucknow, who partnered with Salim Ghouse. Their love story blossomed in Salim's Malabari store, which Reeta-ji visited every evening for bread, eggs and other supplies. The 'improvisation' was touching in its simplicity and tenderness. That was what I remembered when I heard that Reeta-ji had bid adieu to the world on 17 July 2018.

These 'improvisations' were not impromptu acts. The students, and even the teachers, would take weeks to plan and prep for them, keeping the five Ws—who, what, when, where and why—in mind. By the time they took the floor, they were so much in character that they actually lived the role. I remember hearing about Uday, who got so completely involved in his performance that he actually stripped down to his skin. Professor saab, I was told, had allowed him to perform without interrupting because he was mesmerized by the performance. There were times however when he would abruptly cut short an actor and tell him brusquely that he was not being the person, that he was merely 'acting', and he should give the floor to someone else.

Our class boasted some brilliant talents. I still get gooseflesh when I recall Anil's 'improvisation' of a rock star, who after a string of failures, has lost confidence in his talent and turned to substance abuse. Mazhar, who played Anil's manager, takes away his pills and tries to put him back on track. Mazhar was a master of 'improvisation' and I have vivid memories of him as an Air Force pilot who, after having dropped the nuclear bomb on Hiroshima during World War II, is summoned by his superior and instructed to drop a bomb on another Japanese city. He refuses despite knowing that his act of defiance could mean death, brokenly pointing out that he is still haunted by images of young mothers and little children flying in the air, their bodies twisted beyond recognition after the blast. It was incredible the way Mazhar played the guilt-stricken pilot who knows that he has scarred the present generation and perhaps even the future of those who survived the horror. I played his superior and I doff my hat to Professor saab for coming up with such a unique concept and to Mazhar for his emotional intensity.

Rajhans, the guy with the best body in class, once pulled me into his group 'improvisation'. He played my brother-in-law, hiding in our home, and suspicious that I had informed the police, shoots me dead. The shy, conservative girl who played his sister and my wife, whose name unfortunately I fail to recall, underwent a dramatic transformation as I lay 'dead' on her bosom, leaving us dumbstruck with her uninhibited histrionics. Even Professor saab applauded her, but sadly, this wonderful actress faded away into oblivion.

It wasn't easy getting the nod of approval from Professor saab. He demanded 100 per cent involvement from every one of his students, and if any of them were found wanting in their commitment to the course, his criticism was scathing. I got my share of tongue-lashings too, but memories of my father and those

Ramlila days kept me on course. Also, my 'expressive' eyes were a definite asset even back then. Professor saab developed a fondness for me despite the fact that I faltered badly in Geeta Khanna's Bollywood dance classes and the 'movement' class Mithun-da conducted with Phunsukh.

I was born with two left feet and 'movement' was particularly difficult for me. We had to come up with original body movements sparked off by a piece of music, for example '*Lara's theme*' from the 1965 classic *Dr Zhivago*. You couldn't utter a single word during the act, and expression was solely through the fluid movements of the limbs. It was almost like a ballet performance. Mithun-da was the god of 'movement' with his chiselled body and dancing skills, while I was the butt of all jokes. I cringed every second I spent in this particular class. But I didn't dare bunk because I knew if Professor saab ever found out, I could get thrown out of school. Rajesh Mathur, a small-town boy, was the best dancer in our class. Vicky also had a wow physique and excelled in 'movement'. It remains one of the glorious uncertainties of this profession that neither of them made it in showbiz. Ironically, Rajesh is a priest today.

Fortunately, being from the north and thanks to my father, I had an enviable command over both Urdu and Hindi. As a result, both Anil and Mazhar would invite me to their homes on weekends so we could work on our diction, voice modulation and dialogue delivery. Anil also had a harmonium on which we would practise the different scales for voice modulation class.

The classes were long and demanding, stretching from eight in the morning to eight in the evening. After Subhash bhai completed his course at the FTII, he moved to Mumbai and stayed at a PG accommodation behind National College in Bandra and later in Juhu Tara Road near B.R. Chopra's bungalow. These digs offered wholesome meals as well and he invited me to move in with him. I stayed with him for a while.

By the time I got back to our apartment, I would be physically exhausted and mentally drained. I would have a quick bite, prep for the next day's class and then crash. Fortunately, we had the weekends to rejuvenate ourselves because even after opening an acting school in Mumbai, Professor saab's heart was still in Pune. Every Friday, he would return to his home there and come back to the city only on Monday afternoon.

I too missed the warmth of my home and my mother's cooking. I looked forward to visiting Anil's Chembur home, one of the reasons being the delicious ghar ka khana I got there. That's where I also got the first feel of expensive silk when I would change into the freshly laundered lungi and kurta I was handed as soon as I entered. Earlier, I had seen photographs of Kakaji, Rajesh Khanna, wearing similar silk lungi-kurtas onscreen and draping them, I too felt like a superstar.

Shehzad lived next door to Kakaji's iconic bungalow, Aashirwad, in Bandra. He knew everybody in the film industry thanks to Mumtaz-ji. He was also a member of the Sea King Club, which had top-of-the-line billiards tables and hosted competitions that drew all the top actors and film-makers who played the game. For aspiring actors like me, this was the place to be seen and spotted. We would coax Shehzad to get us into the club during these competitions as his guest, despite knowing that we would not be allowed on the billiards floor. He even coaxed Mumtaz-ji to meet several of his classmates from the acting school at his bungalow. That was my first fan-boy moment! What was disturbing though was that Mumtaz-ji didn't believe acting could be taught.

After a year, the course, which turned me from an amateur actor to a serious professional, wound to a close. Professor saab, along with a few teachers and special guests from the industry, judged our final performances, deciding where we stood in class. This was a common practice even at FTII, where Raj Kapoor saab had spotted Shailendra Singh and given him a break as a playback singer in *Bobby*, while Jaya-ji had caught Hrishikesh Mukherjee's eye and been cast in *Guddi*. Anil's father, Surinder Kapoor-uncle, and Sooraj Barjatya's grandfather, Tarachand-ji, were among the invited guests at our acting school that year and we wondered if either of them would spot a star in our midst. Incredibly, the lucky one turned out to be me.

Surinder Kapoor-uncle, whom I had met on many occasions at his residence, complimented Anil and Mazhar warmly, but pronounced that I was the best actor in my class. Tarachand-ji, the founder of Rajshri Productions Pvt. Ltd and the producer of hit family dramas like *Dosti, Jeevan Mrityu, Geet Gaata Chal, Tapasya, Chitchor*, also singled me out and invited me to his office in Prabhadevi. 'Just tell them at the reception that you have come to meet me,' the simple, bespectacled gentleman who was an industry legend told me, little realizing that his words had turned me into a 'hero' among my classmates.

By the end of the day everyone was convinced that I had made it. To be honest, even I believed that Tarachand-ji would offer me a role in one of his films. When I made my way to his office, I was already dreaming of telling my parents that they could stop sending me money orders every month; it was my turn to send money home. On wings of hope, my heart drumming furiously, I waited at the reception wondering if Tarachand-ji would even remember me. He did, and I was immediately escorted to his room. He greeted me warmly and we spoke for a while, but I returned empty-handed.

I went back, again and again, but none of these positive interactions translated into an offer. Perhaps, the reason was that his ghar-parivaar dramas were set in small towns and revolved around characters who were paragons of virtues. Gulshan Grover, with his blazing eyes, deep baritone and intense features, did not fit into the picture. And so, I remained one of the many starry-eyed aspirants in wonderland, wondering if my Bollywood dream would find its way to the silver screen or like Alice, go down some dark labyrinth.

4

DOWN THE ROCKY ROAD

There were frequent letters from my family alerting me that time was fast running out. Even without them reminding me, I knew that if I didn't make it as an actor and stayed too long in a city where I had no future, I would miss out on other opportunities back home in Delhi. With this knowledge hanging over my head like the proverbial Sword of Damocles, I continued walking down my chosen path, but now with some degree of apprehension. Paradoxically, there was also a certain amount of self-assurance because deep down I was confident that I would be able to break into Hindi cinema now that I was a trained actor.

The course at Professor Roshan Taneja's acting school was designed in a way to not just appraise an actor of his strengths and weaknesses, but also to mould him as a person and give him an edge over the competition. When I was undergoing training there, I had discovered that while dance and romance, the primary attributes of a Hindi film hero, were not my forte, with my strong features and the fire burning in my eyes, I excelled in intense roles. While this realization might have alarmed another star aspirant, it boosted my morale. I had not come to Mumbai to become an actor just because everybody in the neighbourhood had raved about my hero-like looks. I had come to the city to make a career in show business, a career that had a long shelf life.

As a student of commerce who had learnt the ABCs of marketing in college, I was aware that easy availability could quickly bring down demand, which is inversely proportional to supply. Since there wasn't a crowd of new faces jostling to become popular villains at the time, I was convinced that I had found my area of expertise that would sustain me over the decades. The only problem was that the Hindi film industry had yet to discover 'Bad Man' Gulshan Grover and so no roles—nayak or khalnayak—were coming my way.

Professor saab, who had always been my pillar of strength, noticed that I was beginning to despair. He came to my rescue, offering me a job as an acting teacher at his institute after I graduated in 1977. I was living in Juhu by then. I shifted in and out of at least ten paying guest accommodations, all of them while being very modest were located conveniently close to the school. I accepted his offer gratefully, knowing it would help me pay my bills and keep me close to the learning process because unlike a conventional teaching job, this one did not require me to only sit behind a desk and spout gyaan. There were times when Professor saab or one of the senior teachers would ask me to take the floor with the students and be a part of an 'improvisation'. This made me feel like a football coach who sometimes takes the field with his players. It made the job not just challenging but also extremely enjoyable.

As an acting teacher, I was part of the training faculty for Sunny Deol, Sanjay Dutt and Kumar Gaurav, along with their leading ladies Tina Munim and Vijayta Pandit. These star sons were being groomed for their big Bollywood launches by their actor–producer fathers, Dharmendra-ji, Sunil Dutt saab and Rajendra Kumar-ji. They had enrolled for special courses, some of which were conducted on the school premises and others in Professor saab's private facility. On occasions, a particular location would be provided for by their parents. In the case

of Sanju, who was to be introduced by Dutt saab in a home
production, *Rocky*, it was in the family's Ajanta Arts Theatre;
while for Kumar Gaurav, popularly called Bunty, who was going
to debut with Rajendra Kumar-ji's *Love Story*, it was the large
private cottage located right behind their Bandra bungalow,
just ahead of Dimple dubbing theatre. So, on one hand, I was
an acting teacher at Professor saab's school, and on the other, a
private instructor to these star kids.

While in a class of twenty-five it is easy to pick and choose
your partners for an 'improvisation', studying in isolation, Sanju,
Sunny, Tina and Bunty had no option but to partner with me
or the female instructor Shehnaaz who accompanied me. This
helped break the ice quickly, so while the other students took
weeks gathering up the courage to ask me to go out with them,
Sanju, in a matter of days, had found out where I lived and would
drive down to pick me up and take me to his Pali Hill bungalow
for dinner.

Dutt saab observed that despite our growing camaraderie,
Sanju listened to my instructions with the respect accorded
to a teacher, and with *Rocky* playing on his mind, requested
Professor saab that he be allowed to watch us in class so he
could gauge just how ready his son was to face the camera.
Happy with the results of the first session, he arranged for
another showing of Sanju's acting chops at the Ajanta Arts
office building. In the audience was Bharat Bhalla saab, who
was writing the script of *Rocky* with Dr Rahi Masoom Reza
saab, cinematographer S. Ramchandra-ji, actor–director
B.S. Thapa-ji, ten to fifteen other team members, and, most
importantly, his mother, Nargis Dutt-ji. Perhaps because he
was performing for the first time in front of so many people,
among them his mother whom he doted on, a nervous Sanju
stumbled momentarily during his act. I quickly brought him
back on track without anyone noticing, or so I believed. But

it didn't escape Dutt saab's eagle eye. Soon after, he called me and offered me a role in *Rocky*.

I was over the moon till I learnt that he wanted me to play Rocky's buddy Jaggi, a comic 'love guru' whose advice comes to nought. I was disappointed because I wanted to play the baddie who murders Rocky's father, distances him from his real mother and puts him on the path of vengeance. But Dutt saab reasoned that as Jaggi I would always be close to Sanju who was playing Rocky, a comforting presence during rehearsals and at the shoot. I accepted his offer and will remain forever grateful to Dutt saab for considering me for such a big film.

Sanju's parents approved of me because they identified with my simple upbringing and liked the fact that I was still untouched by the artifice of a big city. They knew that Sanju was at my place most evenings and preferred it to night-long parties. Only once did I see Dutt saab frown when on asking me for my home number, he learnt that I didn't have a phone at home. Those days it was not easy to get a MTNL connection; you needed to be a Member of Parliament to advocate your case. Even Dutt saab couldn't bring Alexander Graham Bell's invention into my modest digs, but thanks to him I did get my own motorbike.

In the film, Rocky and his friends zoom around on bikes, blithely singing songs. One day, before we began shooting, I was standing with Dutt saab watching Sanju prep for the motorcycle stunts, learning how to balance himself on a bike. He was being coached by the biggest motor cyclist stuntman of the time, 'Kallua' Dilawar Khan. Suddenly his father turned to me and said, 'You should get familiar with a bike too because as Jaggi you will be riding one in the film as well.' I told Dutt saab awkwardly that I didn't have a bike to practise on and to my delight, he promptly bought me one. He even got a few more bikes for the other boys, telling us that we could keep them provided we drove them day and night so that by the time we started shooting we were riding like pros. We were only too happy to oblige.

The motorcycle stunts remind me of a funny incident. Since Sanju's and Bunty's launches were being planned simultaneously, a streak of competitiveness had crept into the two debutants who were neighbours and around the same age. Since I was Bunty's acting coach as well, I cajoled Sanju to invite him over for lunch one afternoon. However, a few days prior to this, Bunty, when asked during an interview if like Sanju he was training in bike riding and taking fight classes, had told a journalist, 'I am an actor, not a stuntman.' I don't think the remark was meant to be derogatory, but the interview appeared on the day of the luncheon and after reading it Sanju vanished, leaving his family and me to entertain Bunty. They eventually became best buddies and took their friendship one step up when Bunty married Sanju's sister Namrata.

Sanju was dating Tina, whom I had first met as a student at the acting school even before *Rocky* started and then as his girlfriend. Like Nargis-ji and Dutt saab, Tina also considered me a stabilizing influence on Sanju who was still a shy, gangly youngster, barely out of his teens. Tina had grown very fond of me and the three of us often went to functions and dinners together. She would also come over to my place occasionally with Sanju for a home-cooked meal. There were times when he would insist on preparing the meal himself to impress her. Sanju is a master of leftovers. Give him some chapattis, dal and curry and he will mash them together in a pan, break in a few eggs, sprinkle some spices, and within minutes, he will have an appetizing meal ready.

Of course, when Tina was there, it couldn't be a meal of leftovers. The master chef would want to prepare some continental chicken dish and would send me a list of exotic ingredients to have ready for him when he arrived at my studio apartment. Incidentally, that studio apartment was bought for me by my parents with their meagre savings. The money was paid with a shower of coins, which had been collected over several years, much to my embarrassment. I know that no matter what I do, I will never be able to repay my family in this lifetime for all that they have done for me.

Getting back to Sanju and his cooking sessions, I had never even heard of some of the ingredients he wanted me to buy, like sour cream and paprika. When I went to the shops looking for them, I discovered that they were expensive firang brands and out of reach of someone who was still counting every rupee. I finally confided to Sanju that I couldn't afford to buy them and laughing good-naturedly, he would go shopping with me, picking them up himself. While cooking, if he asked for some ingredient that had not been on his list, I would point out that I didn't even have a fridge, let alone a well-stocked larder, and that he would have to make do with what was there. It never deterred him. Tina, who came from a large Gujarati family, was very good at rolling out chapattis and roasting them on the stove, which was all my girlfriend Philomina and I could afford back then.

Philomina Lobo and I had met through a common friend. When I bought my first apartment in Krishna building, she moved in with me. My good friend Shashi Ranjan had adopted Philomina as his sister and the three of us were like a family. But every time my parents visited, she had to move out because they didn't know about our relationship. However, the milkman, dhobi and vegetable vendor gave away our secret, asking my mother about the 'other memsaab'. Intrigued, Chaiji turned up one day, unannounced. Philomina, Shashi and I returned home after watching a film to find Chaiji waiting for us. Having discovered that I was in a live-in relationship, she insisted that Philomina was like one of her daughters and pushed us into tying the knot.

I would often hang out with Sanju, Tina, Kintu and Kishore Bajaj and some other friends and have fond memories of those fun evenings. Tina was always a firebrand and already a glamorous star by then, having made her debut with Dev Anand's *Des Pardes* a few years earlier. But coming from a sanskari family, name, fame and money did not go to her head. She remained a sensible, balanced person who had a big hand in grooming Sanju, me and others around her. Sadly, her contribution to Sanju's stardom has gone largely unacknowledged, even in Rajkumar Hirani's biopic, *Sanju*. Even back then, though Sanju was wooing her ardently, and was part of Tina's group which included her sister Bhavana and brother-in-law Dr Tushar Motiwala, her secretary, Kaka, her executive assistant, Meena Iyer, her best friends Kintu and Kishore, he refused to acknowledge their relationship in front of his parents and the world. This led to frequent and heated spats between the two.

On one such occasion, I was excited about attending a star-studded New Year's bash at Sanju's bungalow, and so I borrowed money to buy myself some new clothes. Spiffily dressed, I made my way there. Just as I was about to enter, I saw Tina storming out. Spotting me, she dragged me away with her, saying urgently, 'Come, let's go.' Knowing that Tina was angry and upset, I lost all interest in the party. The only thought I had was how to make things right for my friend and sister. Suddenly, she noticed that Sanju had run out of the house too and knowing he would come after her, Tina hopped on my bike and instructed me to drive. I hit the accelerator and we zoomed off. I didn't ask her about her abrupt exit. She asked me, 'Where is Philomina?' When I told her that she was at the apartment, Tina suggested we go there and have our own New Year celebration. I took her home, Philomina rustled up some dinner for all of us and we brought in the New Year together.

I drove her back to her Khar residence at around four in the morning. Just as I turned into her lane, I noticed Sanju and his cousin Gopal Bali. They had almost passed out on the pavement from exhaustion. The roar of the bike alerted Sanju and he got to his feet wearily and looked at us. For a moment I wondered if he would get into a scuffle with me for having whisked away his girlfriend to God knows where. Tina has always been like a sister to me and to his credit, Sanju did not misunderstand, not even in that exhausted, frazzled state. For almost seven hours he had been worrying about what had happened to her because while her car and chauffeur had returned home, Tina had gone missing after their altercation. He must have imagined all kinds of nightmarish scenarios and was relieved to find that she had been with my wife and me all the time. He cried and apologized profusely to her. Tina invited him into her house, along with me, and we brought in the New Year again, this time with Sanju. They eventually broke up and Tina married industrialist Anil Ambani, a wonderful person with a large heart, who respects his wife and gives her the dignity that is her due. Men like Anil Ambani are rare.

Tina and I had one big misunderstanding. Ranjeet, a senior actor, was getting married. Dutt saab and Nargis-ji were doing the kanyadaan. It was a big fat Bollywood wedding and I was excited as I made my way towards Ranjeet's bungalow, which was right next to Sanjay Khan saab's home in Juhu, with Tina and Sanju in the same car. We got out of the car together. As Tina wanted to adjust her sari, she thrust the gift she had brought along into my hands.

I was just a struggling actor then, not a big name like Tina or Sanju. I was also not very well off, which was evident from my clothes. I was wearing a shirt and trousers while Sanju was in an expensive suit and Tina in a designer sari. I told them that if I walked in carrying this gift, I would look like their chamcha, a hanger-on, rather than their friend. I handed the box back to Tina and stomped off. I realize today that I overreacted because her intention had not been to belittle me. I didn't meet Tina for many days after this incident till she bridged the gap, telling me reproachfully that she had not set out to humiliate me. She had given the box to me only because she was afraid Sanju might drop it and the expensive gift inside might break. It was water under the bridge for me by then and we quickly became the best of friends once again.

Today, even though she is the Ambani bahu, she is still the same old Tina with me. She sails into my apartment building occasionally for a home-cooked meal, with her security guards and entourage of cars, but she has no airs and is unmindful of gawking neighbours. It takes me back to the good old days. My living room, fortunately, has received the nod of approval from her, except for a false partition bisecting the room, behind which there's a television set and a photo gallery of my significant moments. Every time she drops by, she knocks on the wood and says disapprovingly, 'This must go.'

Tina was always very close to her father Nandkumar-ji and has a deep concern for the elderly. In 2004, she started the Harmony for Silvers Foundation, an NGO that strives to enhance the quality of life for senior citizens. Every year, unless I'm out of the country, I stand by her side and flag off the Harmony Senior Citizen's Run, proud to have this wonderful and vibrant woman as my friend. Over the years, Tina's warmth and effervescence remain unchanged. When Steven Spielberg was in Mumbai, I was invited to a party hosted in honour of the Oscar-winning film-maker at the Ambani residence. Soon after my arrival, Tina called out to Spielberg and introduced me as one of her closest friends, asking the photographer to take a picture of the three of us together.

Tina is the chairperson of the Mumbai-based Kokilaben Hospital, and while this multi-speciality hospital was being built, she would share the plans with me. Talking of hospitals, I'm reminded of the time my father was undergoing a surgery. I was just beginning to rise as an actor then and had stopped visiting the Dutts because of my work commitments. One day, I spotted Dutt saab at the airport and rushed to take his blessings. 'Where are you off to?' he asked me, and I told him that I was flying to Delhi to be with my father who was to be operated on the next day. He asked me which hospital Pitaji had been admitted to and told me not to worry. 'God is with us and will give us strength,' he reassured.

I reached the hospital to find my father looking disturbed and a deeply concerned Chaiji in tears. Those days, doctors didn't believe in confiding in patients and their families, and this added to our tension. I was trying to reassure them that the surgery would go off well when I heard a commotion in the corridor. I looked up and to my surprise saw Dutt saab walk in with a group of twenty people, which included the hospital's best doctors, trustees, members of his staff and his security guards. He came straight to my father's bed and, talking to my parents in Punjabi, soothed their fears. At his words, I saw a relieved smile light up Chaiji's face. Then, after consulting with the doctors, Dutt saab left, unmindful of the starry-eyed patients and hospital staff.

In those days it was unthinkable for a movie star—Dutt saab was also a well-known film-maker—to visit the general ward of a hospital to enquire after the health of a struggling actor's father. But Dutt saab and Nargis-ji always treated me like an elder son while Sanju's sisters, Namrata and Priya, tied rakhis on my wrist for years. Dutt saab's affection never diminished till the very end.

My father went into the operation theatre the next day with a smile on his face. We waited outside knowing he would get the best medical care possible thanks to Dutt saab's unexpected visit. As Dutt saab had predicted, Pitaji was soon back home, hale and hearty. I never forgot his heart-warming gesture.

It was at Dutt saab's Pali Hill bungalow where I first met many of Bollywood's who's who when I was invited for dinner. I would pinch myself to be sure that I was sharing the table with Gulshan Rai, the veteran distributor and producer who had launched the careers of scriptwriters Salim Khan and Javed Akhtar with films like *Deewaar* and *Trishul*. The only thing we had in common was our name, Gulshan. But while his garden was blooming with flowers like *Johny Mera Naam* and *Joshila*, in mine you couldn't even spot a stray bud.

Other guests at these dinners were the legendary Dilip Kumar and Saira Banu-ji, Asha Parekh and Shammi-ji. Dilip saab was someone whose name I had grown up revering but whom I had only seen onscreen. To see him in person, sitting beside me, to be conversing with him on a variety of subjects, made me feel like the star which I wasn't at the time.

Almost a decade later, in the action-drama *Kanoon Apna Apna*, both Sanju and I got to share the screen with Dilip saab. He played a district collector and Sanju was his cop son. Needless to say, I was the baddie. Sanju and I were inseparable during the shooting in Chennai, hanging out together at all hours. Since Dilip saab was Sanju's neighbour and family friend, he was very protective of him and affectionate towards me too, advising us on how certain scenes needed to be played out. He was staying in the same hotel as we were and every evening after pack-up, he would summon us and narrate anecdotes from his heydays. While these stories were fascinating, Sanju and I were both young and eager to go out and party with the girls. There was no way we could take Dilip saab into confidence, so the only way out was to slip away before his call came. After that we knew there was no way for him to connect with us since there were no cell phones at the time.

This called for careful planning and strategizing. Dilip saab was in the habit of strolling in the corridor every evening. The only way to escape his eagle eye was to duck into the elevator the minute he turned the corner. One evening, I had made my escape but while Sanju was about to get into the elevator, Dilip saab's voice rang out from down the corridor, '*Beta, kahan jaa rahe ho*? Where are you off to in such a tearing hurry? Come, let's go to my room and chat for a while.' And with that, it was goodnight for Sanju!

5

RK TO SK

Rocky and Sanju's launch was delayed when Nargis-ji was diagnosed with pancreatic cancer. Her illness and Sanju's own battle with drugs meant that the film was in the making for a long time. During this period, I survived in Mumbai only thanks to the benevolence of Professor Roshan Taneja saab who had grown really fond of me by then. He let me take three classes a day at his acting school so I could make ends meet. The classes increased over time and the extra money helped me live better than I would otherwise have.

As mentioned earlier, Surinder Kapoor-uncle was very impressed with me after watching my performance at the acting school and graciously allowed me to hang out at his office in Famous Studio, Mahalaxmi, where every big producer had their offices too. Every day, around noon, he would drive down there from his Chembur home with his sons, Boney and Anil. I would be waiting for them at the turning in Mahim and as they drove up, I would jump into the car and spend the day with Anil. We would visit the offices of producers and studios. Occasionally, I would go into town with Anil when he went to meet Sunita, his wife, whom he was dating back then.

Occasionally Surinder Kapoor-uncle would walk me to the offices of some of the other producers. To a struggler like me, all

44

of them looked like a movie break, but without my large-hearted mentor, I might as well have stood outside their door for months, trying to persuade the peon to give me five minutes with the manager. If I was lucky, someone would accept my photographs only to push them into the nearest drawer as soon as I turned my back. And out of sight is out of mind!

F.C. Mehra saab was a well-known producer and a big name at the time who also owned Minerva theatre in Mumbai and Plaza cinema in Delhi. His banner, Eagle Films, had produced Shammi Kapoor saab's romcom *Professor*, Sunil Dutt saab and Vyjayanthimala-ji's historical drama *Amrapali* and Raaj Kumar-ji's *Lal Patthar*. He had also produced popular sitcoms like *Zabaan Sambhalke* and *Office Office*. Surinder Kapoor-uncle recommended me strongly to Mehra saab, telling him and his sons, Umesh-ji and Rajiv, that I was a fantastic actor. And that's how I bagged *Ek Jaan Hain Hum*, Rajiv's directorial debut. Umesh Mehra-ji also changed my life, casting me in every film of his.

Ek Jaan Hain Hum, a campus romance, introduced another Rajiv, Raj Kapoor saab's son and Randhir and Rishi's younger brother. Opposite Rajiv Kapoor, fondly called Chimpu, was newcomer Divya Rana. The film also featured another debutante, Kiran Vairale, along with veteran actors like Chimpu's uncle Shammi Kapoor-ji, Pran saab, Tanuja-ji and Rakesh Bedi. I was elated to be cast as the main villain. When a film star's son is being launched, every little detail is run by the patriarch. For Raj Kapoor saab to vet me and not find me wanting was a huge high. I knew all the who's who of Bollywood would turn up to see Raj Kapoor saab's son and I prayed that I would catch their eye too.

While we were working on the film, Chimpu and I became friends. It was a real thrill to be invited to the annual Holi bash at RK Studio, which I had only read about in magazines. I was a thin, young boy whom nobody knew at the time. I was almost turned away from the gate till Chimpu came out and reassured the guards that I was a fellow actor. They let me in, somewhat reluctantly, and I stepped into the iconic studio, feeling privileged. We played with colours, I was dunked in the pool as was the custom, before I crossed the threshold and stepped into RK Cottage, coming face to face with the legendary Raj Kapoor saab. In the company of the man I had grown up idolizing, I didn't feel like an outsider any more. The years of struggle didn't weigh so heavily on my shoulders. Suddenly, there was something to write home about.

Meanwhile, Boney Kapoor was in the process of taking over the reins of the family banner, SK Films, and was getting ready to flag off his first production. *Hum Paanch* was the Hindi remake of the Kannada film *Paduvaaralli Pandavaru*, which told the story of the five Pandavas in a rural set-up in the modern age. In the film, Sanjeev Kumar saab played Krishna, Shabana Azmi-ji was Sundariya and Naseer (Naseeruddin Shah) enacted the role of Suraj. Raj Babbar was cast as Arjun and Mithun-da was Bhima while Amrish Puri-ji's character, Vir Pratap Singh, was modelled on Duryodhan. Shabana-ji had strongly recommended Uday from the FTII while Mithun-da was backing another actor for the role of the fifth Pandava. As Mithun-da's star was on the ascendant, his choice may well have prevailed had it not been for Surinder Kapoor-uncle.

One day, Boney's father called, saying he wanted to meet me. He asked me straightaway if I had a problem with Mithun. Baffled, I shook my head, informing him that Mithun-da had been my teacher at Professor saab's acting school and we had remained good friends ever since. 'Then why is he recommending another actor for Mahavir? Make him understand that you are the best choice for this role,' Surinder Kapoor-uncle insisted.

I didn't think twice. I dashed off to where Mithun-da was shooting, asking him not to deprive me of a lifetime's chance.

Baffled by my fervent pleas, Mithun-da told me that he had no idea I was also in the running for the same role and assured me that he would not stand in my way.

But one more problem emerged. Shabana-ji has a light complexion, while I am tanned. There were misgivings about whether I would look like her brother. This time she came to my rescue, giving me the nod. And that is how I ended up playing the fifth brother in *Hum Paanch*. It was such an important role that when *Rocky*'s shoot overlapped with Boney's schedule, I had to request Dutt saab to help me out. He eventually shot a few of my scenes with a duplicate. The films released within months of each other, *Hum Paanch* on 27 November 1980 and *Rocky* on 26 April 1981.

We shot *Hum Paanch* in Melukote, a quaint little town 50 kilometres from Mysore and the hometown of Tamil Nadu's former chief minister J. Jayalalithaa. Melukote was not equipped for a large film unit. Unfazed, Boney built fourteen cottages for his actors and technical heads. The rest of his staff were put up in dorms. He even constructed a community kitchen and had eighteen cooks flown down and pulled a telephone line from nearby Mandya so the unit could stay connected with their families. He also took along a 16-mm projector to screen movies after pack-up as there was nothing else to do in this quiet little town whose only landmark was the famous Cheluvanarayana Swamy Temple.

Anil Kapoor, a hero in waiting at the time, was helping Boney with the production. He would occasionally drive down to Bengaluru to accompany a star from the airport. Whenever he was in Melukote, we would discuss my scenes between shots and at times he even rehearsed them with me. Once, Anil and I went to see an English film, whose name I don't remember, with Shabana-ji. That was the first time I was watching a film with someone from the industry whom I had long admired. I kept stealing glances at her all through the film to see what impact the emotions being projected onscreen had on another actor.

Soon after, Anil got his big break in the Telugu film, *Vamsa Vruksham*, followed by *Woh 7 Din*, another Bapu directorial and a Boney Kapoor production. Boney asked me to face the camera for good luck and the film has a passing shot of me walking past.

After *Hum Paanch*, Raj Babbar, Amrish Puri-ji, Shabana-ji and Mithun-da started recommending me to their producers, which was really nice of them. I would land a small role in their films, shoot for a week, then, be without work for months. Shashi Ranjan, Mazhar Khan and a few other friends would also hang out at Mehboob Studio, looking for acting jobs. Shashi would occasionally take me along for dinner at the cottage of actress Priya Rajvansh and legendary film-maker Chetan Anand saab. What an experience it was to spend time with them!

But such highs were few and far between. I vividly remember those endless months of struggle when I would spend hours trying to frame my daily letters to my parents because there was nothing significant to write about. But I couldn't let my frustration spill on to the paper, knowing it would only worry them. I couldn't not write either because I knew my letters were the highpoint of their life. If for some reason the postman didn't arrive, they wouldn't sleep, and on occasions, my anxious parents have gone knocking on the dakiya babu's door late at night, entreating him to go through his post bag one more time to see if my letter was not tucked inside somewhere.

Once or twice, the postman babu had dropped my letter through the window or had slid it under the door and it had slipped out of sight. My father would push aside the bed and the steel almirah, check behind and under every bit of furniture in the room, looking for the letter till someone pulled it out with a lot of effort. After this happened a few times, the postman babu was requested to deliver the letter personally to my parents who always welcomed him with a cup of tea. After I became a star, during my short visits home, there was a long list of people I was expected to meet with his name right at the top.

Those were dark days and I was beginning to despair when I ran into Anil who asked me if I would be interested in doing a regional film. I was so desperate for work that I told him I was ready for anything. With a wry smile, he told me to come along with him to Ooty. He said that the producer had even sent a flight ticket for me. I was delighted till he told me, while driving in through the hotel gates, that seeing me so depressed he had bought my ticket himself and brought me along. He thought it would be a change of scene for me and pointed out that I could stay with him and help him rehearse his scenes. It was a heart-warming gesture but at that moment, I was reduced to being a part of the hero's entourage. I was shocked and aghast!

Anil dashed out of the car before I could explode. I took my time stepping out and, still seething, walked into the hotel lobby where I ran into several south Indian gentlemen I had never met before. As Anil introduced me to them, I shook hands, even as anger bubbled inside me, making my eyes more bloodshot than usual. I guess, my eyes caught the attention of Mani Ratnam's director of photography, Balu Mahendra. Oblivious of his interest, I took the elevator up to Anil's suite which I was now expected to share with him. I waited impatiently for him to arrive so I could confront him. When he finally walked in, Mani and Balu were with him and I had to clamp down on my temper.

I later learnt that after my stormy exit, Balu had drawn Anil aside and told him that I had an interesting face and eyes that were spitting fire. He wondered if I could act. Anil informed him that we had been classmates at the acting school and convinced him that I was a fabulous actor. On Anil's insistence, the renowned cinematographer, editor, director and writer of Tamil cinema offered me the role of the bad man in his first Hindi film. Written and directed by Balu himself, *Sadma* was a remake of his Tamil film *Moondram Pirai*, a beautiful love story with Kamal Haasan and Sridevi in the lead. It had music by Ilaiyaraaja sir and lyrics by Gulzar saab. It was a lucky break for me, and I grabbed the offer even before I had heard the story or knew about all the big names associated with the project. I was just so happy and relieved to have landed a role in a film.

But being a producer himself, Anil understood that no matter how much the director liked me, the producer had to confirm me first for me to do the film. So, he persuaded Balu to ring up Romu N. Sippy, who along with his brother Raj N. Sippy was producing this film, and inform him that Gulshan Grover would be playing the baddie, Balua. Romu was surprised because they had signed another actor, a bigger name, for the role. But Balu was adamant he wanted only me. Romu, a legendary and a gentlemanly producer of films like *Mere Apne, Koshish* and *Achanak*, spoke to me on the phone and wanted us to meet immediately so we could work out the formalities. The next day, I flew back to Mumbai after being repeatedly warned by Balu not to shave because he wanted Balua to look rough and dishevelled. I promised him that I wouldn't shave all my life if needed. He wanted me to grow out my hair and I vowed that I wouldn't cut it for the next two years. Everyone laughed at my sincerity.

I met the very suave Romu at his office in Rooptara Studio. He welcomed me warmly and we signed the contract that very day. He even gave me a much-needed advance and I was back in the race. I take this opportunity to express my gratitude to my friend Anil Kapoor because of whom I found myself in the company of the Sippy brothers, producer and director Romu and Raj, who, in later years, would change my career forever.

6

SOUTH-SIDE STORY

A day or two into the shoot of *Sadma* in Ooty, a few suggestions I offered impressed Balu Mahendra so much that he handed the dialogue file to me and told me that now I had the job of coaching Kamal Haasan, Sridevi and Silk Smitha to speak Hindi with the right accent and pronunciation. I couldn't refuse my director, so with great reluctance I took over from a lady who had been my senior in the Little Theatre Group in Delhi as the film's official dialogue supervisor.

Kamal and Sridevi were a delight to be with during my interactions with them over their dialogues. Silk Smitha was one of the busiest stars at the time. Rarely was a film down south made without her in a special appearance. She would fly down to the location, drive directly to the hotel from the airport, freshen up before coming on set, wrap up her scenes in a jiffy and zip off to the next project. On the day she was to arrive for our shoot, I was left behind at the hotel so I could narrate her scenes and go over her lines with her before she was driven to the set. I don't think she realized that I was also one of the actors till the movie's release. Her staff treated me like an assistant director and made me sit outside her room for hours. Silk Smitha herself was always respectful, but not really interested in what I was saying. I don't know how much Hindi I managed to teach her.

It was a unit of wonderfully talented and very warm actors and technicians, headed by our gentlemanly producer Romu Sippy who was there throughout the shoot. Kamal, Sridevi and Balu would often jabber away in Tamil on the set even when I was around them. Then, noticing the blank look on my face, they would abruptly stop and Kamal would translate all that had been said in English with Balu urging me to learn some Tamil so they wouldn't have to go through this tedious process every day. Kamal, who would go jogging every evening with Romu and me, succeeded in teaching me a smattering of Tamil and also how to handle our fight scenes, since I was very nervous about them. From him, I learnt the technique of overpowering an actor who was far bigger and stronger than me convincingly onscreen. His tips came with dollops of humour. 'So, you first do this, then, you do this [demonstrating with actions]. Come now, you know how it's done. Yes, that's right, you got it. Now, throw in a punch like this. I know by the time we are done with this scene, you will come to hate me so much that after the shoot you will want to tear a picture of mine to shreds, right?'

I had an equally wonderful equation with Sridevi, even though she was very shy, right up to her untimely death in 2018. The only time I got nervous in her presence was when we were filming the scene where my character, Balua, attempts to molest her. Even though I was a trained actor and had been an acting teacher as well, I had never been called upon to do a rape scene before; it is also something that cannot be taught in class. Also, the very act of forcing myself on a woman is repugnant to me. I had grown up around my mother and my sisters and learnt to respect every woman who crossed my path. So, when I had to 'act' contrary to my nature and upbringing, it made me anxious.

My costume was old and hadn't been washed in six months. When I stepped out in it on the day of the shoot, Romu, whose two-bedroom suite I was sharing, wrinkled his nose in disgust at the stench that emanated from me. He instructed me to dab some cologne so I wouldn't stifle Sridevi with my foul-smelling presence. I did as he asked and we left for the set together. En route, we ran into Kamal who took one look at my ashen complexion and quipped, 'So, today is your big scene, huh?' Romu guffawed but all I could manage was a nervous titter.

Romu told Kamal and Balu about the cologne and there was much amusement on the set. As soon as Balu shouted, 'Lights, Camera, Action!' I lunged for Sridevi. Completely in character, she pushed me away so hard I landed in a heap on the floor several feet away. There was a roar of laughter from Kamal and Romu and with a hurried 'Cut' Balu came running towards me. He looked at me, sitting there looking stupefied, and said with a straight face, 'What is this? The mighty villain has fallen!' I quickly recovered my equilibrium and was back on my feet. The second take went off smoothly and we wrapped up the scene quickly, thanks to Sridevi. Without saying it in so many words, she made me realize just how important it was to enact a rape scene without hurting the dignity of my female co-star.

Every actress resents and detests a strange man touching her. I don't remember her exact words, but the gist of what Sridevi told me that day was that while projecting a certain emotion, I had to be careful not to make the object of my lust feel uncomfortable with my unwelcome attention. I had to ensure that no matter what, I was never out of line. That was the biggest lesson I learnt on the sets of *Sadma*, and one which I have diligently practised all through my career.

In later years, in an interesting turn of events, given that I would make their lives hell onscreen, several heroines, from Rekha-ji, Anita Raj to Kimi Katkar, Dimple Kapadia, Manisha Koirala, Raveena Tandon, Tabu, Karisma Kapoor and Mahima Chaudhry often pushed their producers to sign me because I never inconvenienced them in scenes that demanded physical proximity.

Mahima has been a very dear friend for years. I met her during a Bollywood world concert tour which also featured Akshay Kumar and Suniel Shetty among others. We got along fabulously and I hung out with her sister Ash and her. We watched movies together, went pub hopping, visited nightclubs and took off on shopping sprees. Mahima arranged for me to visit the United Nations and made it a memorable trip. She is a beautiful, warm and caring woman, a delight to spend time with.

During this time, she was doing a film in which she falls in love with a younger man and her jealous husband kills her after he learns about the affair. Initially, the idea was that a top hero would be roped in to play the part of her husband, but after meeting and interacting with me, Mahima insisted that it should be me, reasoning that it would be a surprise casting. The director wondered out aloud if Mahima, a Subhash Ghai discovery and a top actress at the time, was sure she wanted to play a 'villain's' wife. She laughed and told him that she would be happy for me to join the team, pointing out that despite my 'Bad Man' image 'Gulshan is sweetheart, a wonderful person and colleague'.

Here, I must mention that though Mahima is not fond of this film, it gave me a friend for life. Although both of us are very opinionated, and hold strong views, we have never had any differences except for one occasion when we got into a heated argument—at the birthday party of our close friend, businessman Navin Luther. But that was, I suspect, the handiwork of my dear actor friend Suniel Shetty, whose practical joke was behind that particular episode.

Suniel and I, along with Jackie Shroff, Arbaaz Khan and Mahima, are regulars at Navin's annual birthday bash in the capital. And whenever we are together, we have a blast though Suniel, the prankster that he is, has on occasions got me into trouble with his mischief. Even now, I'm always wary of his calls when I am en route to the airport, informing me that my flight is a couple of hours late. As I begin to panic, lightning strikes. I call back to find out if we are booked on the same flight, and the game is up for Suniel. It's thanks to buddies like him that life continues to be a fun ride.

Suniel, with whom I have worked in more than a dozen films—including *Dilwale*, *Mohra*, *Hera Pheri*, *Dus* and *Red Alert: The War Within*—has been one of my closest buddies and supporters in this journey. Every time Suniel, a successful businessman besides a popular actor, starts a new venture, he calls to offer me a partnership. His affection extends to my son too. For Suniel and his dear wife Mana, Sanjay is as much their child as Athiya and Ahan.

Talking about Suniel reminds me of a family I am very close to, the Wigs of Rohtak, a family of industrialists and philanthropists. Mahima, Suniel, Mana bhabhi and I are always there at sports marathons and events organized by the Wigs. And whether I am running a marathon, playing table tennis at the Wigs' Micron Table Tennis Academy or at a dinner at their home, I rely on Mana bhabhi and Mahima to save me from another of Suniel's pranks.

It makes me very happy to be getting back on the sets with Suniel, on the gangster drama *Mumbai Saga*, more so because it is directed by Sanjay Gupta. It is the awesome Gupps who made me realize how a small role, in *Aatish*, can make such a big impact only because of the way he shot it and made me perform. And that continued with films like *Kaante*, *Acid Factory* and others. Now I'm looking forward to *Mumbai Saga*.

Like Mahima, Dimple, with whom I had worked earlier in *Ram Lakhan* and *Leela*, also suggested my name for the role of her lover in *Chehre: A Modern Day Classic*, after listening to the narration, echoing Mahima's opinion that I would give the story an interesting twist and because she felt at ease in my company. Dimple eventually didn't do the film for some reason, but Manisha, who stepped in, was equally excited about the casting for precisely the same reasons. To date, Mahima and Manisha are my everyday buddies, with whom I can go out for a film or a bite.

In the West, leading actresses have a clause in their contracts that if a scene requires kissing and intimacy, the actor cast opposite them would be signed with their consent. We don't have such clauses in Bollywood, but it is important for the leading lady to be comfortable with her male co-stars. It surprised many film-makers when my name came up time and again as the chosen one. For me, it only reaffirmed what Sridevi had taught me: to respect a woman who shared the screen with me. My fraternity respected me for my sincerity, hard work and the sanskar my parents had instilled in me. Like the ladies in the kothis in Delhi to whom I would sell household supplies as a young boy, Bollywood's heroines also gave their thumbs up to this 'gentleman actor' and their recommendations went a long way in furthering my career.

I was one of the few Hindi film villains who got to romance the leading lady in a song in K.C. Bokadia's *Shaktiman*. Bokadia-ji was extremely fond of me and, like Romu Sippy after *Sadma*, cast me in every film he produced. There were occasions when he wouldn't even bother to narrate a script. He would simply tell me that he planned to start shooting from Sunday with Dharmendra-ji and me. 'Sir, please be there,' I was instructed, and it was understood that I would be there. No questions asked.

The shoot for *Shaktiman* started in snow-covered Manali on New Year's Eve in 1992 with Karisma Kapoor and Ajay Devgn in the lead. Ajay is the son of action–director Veeru Devgan-ji, with whom I had worked in *Shiva Ka Insaaf*. Veeru-ji was like a father figure who had really helped me in the early stages of my career and Ajay was very fond of me, right from our first film. One of my films with Ajay was Salim Akhtar's *Jigar* and one of the dialogues in that film (*'Yeh inspector zara duja kisam ke hain'*) became extremely popular. Despite the biting cold, the Manali schedule went off smoothly and we flew back to Mumbai to shoot a romantic song with Ajay and Karisma. Bokadia-ji suddenly shocked everyone by announcing that he wanted to film the song on Karisma and me. 'But Gulshan is the bad man, sir,' his flabbergasted team pointed out, and he replied, 'That's the beauty of it!'

Naach-gaana has never been my forte. Even in acting school, I had dreaded dance and 'movement' classes as my hands and feet were never in sync. The fear was so deep-rooted that I even turned down a film because it required me to dance. My mentor Shabana Azmi-ji had recommended me for the role of her son in Dasari Narayan Rao's *Aaj Ka M.L.A. Ram Avtar.* The film was launched in Chennai and she even got me a plane ticket so I could fly down for the mahurat and familiarize myself with the way film-makers worked down south. I met the team, liked their warmth and professionalism, but terrified that a full song was to be picturized on me, when I couldn't even pull off three steps, opted out.

This was back in the 1980s and conscious of my Achilles heel, I started discussing my weakness with several legendary actors in the hope that I would find a way to better myself. When I confided in him, Kaka-ji told me not to worry too much and revealed that he had developed his signature move when grooving to one of his chartbusters as a way of covering up for something he was not comfortable or confident about. 'Many a time I don't remember the lines of a song. So, despite my best efforts, I often find it difficult to lip sync properly. One of my choreographers eventually suggested I roll both my hands and cover my lips with them because lip sync is a must during a song. Who would have believed that it would become one of my biggest aces,' admitted the 'Phenomenon', Rajesh Khanna-ji.

Dharmendra-ji also confessed that he found it hard to fall in step with the dance director. 'After several retakes, I suggested that they play the music and just let me do what came naturally to me. Luckily, the ploy worked. To this day I am unable to repeat a step because I don't know how I did it in the first place,' Paaji guffawed.

These conversations were reassuring, because unlike the message inherent in the title of the Remo D'Souza-directed hit franchise, *ABCD: Any Body Can Dance*, I believe that if you are not a born dancer, you can never perfect the art. The way out is to evolve your own style. By the time the song in *Shaktiman*, '*Haule haule dil doongi*', was shot, success had brought along a self-assurance of its own. I also had an understanding choreographer in Kamal Master-ji who gave me fairly easy steps with the focus being on the romantic portions. We flew to Chennai and flitting from one elaborate set to another, with several costume changes and an extremely encouraging and wonderful co-star in Karisma who helped me so much, I was able to pull off the song without too much trouble. I loved every minute of playing the lover boy but was equally happy to get back to my bad ways.

I thought my brush with song, dance and romance had ended with *Shaktiman*, but surprisingly, I got to romance the heroine again in Romu's *Amaanat*. The action flick, directed by his brother Raj Sippy whom we affectionately called Daddu-ji, featured Sanjay Dutt in the lead with Akshay Kumar in the supporting role of his friend. I played a dashing, sexy playboy whom Heera Rajagopal is married off to when they are both kids. After that, my parents move to the city and I forget all about my child bride. So, when the orphaned village belle turns up at my doorstep claiming to be my wife, I drive her out. She is saved from committing suicide by the two do-gooders who take her home to their chawl and groom her into a stunning princess, promising her that one day soon, her husband, who had disowned her, would be drawn to her.

Daddu-ji had incorporated a song, '*Ho gaya ji ho gaya*', in which I had to passionately woo Heera. Believing me to be her husband, she is happy to be seduced. Only Sanjay, who has fallen in love with her, and his buddy, Akshay, are desperate to stop me from having my way with her. Most baddies have been a part of many item numbers in which they are treated with equal measures of humour and terror, but few can claim to have romanced their leading ladies in the way the hero does. I can proudly say that this bad man did it, in *Amaanat* and many other films.

My south-side story won't be complete without mentioning my friend Pradeep Sharma, who is married to Padmini Kolhapure. Tutu, as he is fondly called, is a successful producer and was a part of a large group of friends, which included Umesh Mehra-ji, Jeetendra-ji, Mazhar Khan, Manoj K.T., Indra Kumar, Ashok Thakeria, Boney Kapoor and Shashi Ranjan. I grew close to them and Tutu took it upon himself to help this struggling actor. Thanks to Jeetu-ji, Tutu was very close to many film-makers in the south and got me a role in the Hindi remake of the Telugu super-hit, *Nyayam Kavali*. Titled *Mujhe Insaaf Chahiye*, the film was directed by T. Rama Rao Garu and the story was about a young girl played by Rati Agnihotri. Tutu got me the role of her boyfriend. He described it as a 'different hero's role' and though I was scared of offending him, I turned it down saying I didn't want to play a hero. So, Mithun-da was signed for it.

Undeterred, the ever-helpful Tutu then brought me *Ek Nai Paheli,* directed by K. Balachander-ji who had also helmed the Tamil original *Apoorva Raagangal* and the super-hit *Ek Duuje Ke Liye.* The film featured Raaj Kumar saab, Hema Malini-ji and Padmini. 'It's an important role and the film is being produced by Subba Rao who is really big down south. You even have romantic scenes with Hema-ji,' Tutu informed me proudly and was shocked when with folded hands I turned down this offer too, repeating that I didn't want to play a hero. This role went to Kamal Haasan.

Tutu, who continued to be a pillar of support, then sounded me out on *Naache Mayuri*, the Hindi remake of T. Rama Rao Garu's Telugu film *Mayuri*. It marked Sudha Chandran's acting debut and revolved around a classical dancer who loses her leg, but not her will, in an accident. I couldn't refuse another film by T. Rama Rao Garu outright, so I met him and explained that I was averse to playing the hero. 'But this hero betrays the girl,' he argued. I had been told by many colleagues that it was an offer not to be missed, yet I still told him that I couldn't do it. As soon as I left his office, I called and informed my friends Shehzad Askari, Shashi Ranjan and Shekhar Suman about the role. It was eventually bagged by Shashi Ranjan who shot for *Naache Mayuri* for three days before he made way for Shekhar.

Tutu almost gave up on me after I turned down these three big films. However, I then learnt about another film by T. Rama Rao Garu, the social drama *Yeh Desh,* which was the Hindi remake of actor Krishna's 200th Telugu film *Eenadu.* I chased Tutu to get me a role in that film. I even took help from Shashi Ranjan to convince Tutu and the three of us went to Bhalla Bungalow on Pali Hill where Jeetu-ji was shooting. He is always a pleasure to be with and was invariably helpful to struggling actors. When Tutu told him that he thought I was best suited to play the role of his son, Jeetu-ji spoke to T. Rama Rao Garu and I was signed on. Parveen Babi-ji played my mother till she suddenly left the industry and was replaced by Zeenat Aman-ji. The film also had Kamal as Inspector Mathur.

Back then, I used to live in an apartment in Krishna building which is close to the ISKCON temple in Juhu. One day, when I was at the nearby baniya shop making a call, I noticed a guy in dark glasses grooving to music playing on his Walkman. He stared back and I muttered, 'Kamal?' He ignored me and continued to dance. I repeated myself, and this time he shushed me, and taking me aside asked, 'How did you recognize me?' I smiled and told the legendary Kamal Haasan, 'I'm an actor too, I can recognize body language.'

Coincidentally, I had just run into my other *Sadma* co-star Sridevi outside Seth Studio where she was shooting for Rakesh Roshan's *Jaag Utha Insan*. She was sniffling, and so, I enquired after her health and she told me that it was freezing inside. Seth Studio was the only air-conditioned studio in Mumbai at the time and I guess they had upped the temperature so that producers would get their money's worth, thereby turning it into an Artic zone. When I informed Kamal that Sridevi was also in Mumbai, he insisted that I take him to her hotel. We went up to her floor together, he still in disguise. He told me that he would barge into her room pretending to be a foreigner. Kamal has a fantastic sense of humour and having done several films with Sridevi in the south, he knew her well enough to play pranks on her. But I have never been a prankster, and even though I knew that they were friends, I was worried about Sridevi's reaction. I heaved a sigh of relief when we discovered that she was not in her room.

I also worked with the superstar of superstars, Rajinikanth, in films like *Mahaguru*, *Insaaf Kaun Karega* and *Tyagi*. He is a class actor and a perfect gentleman. In 2017, I met him at the wedding reception of Shatrughan Sinha-ji's son Kush. I am usually one of the early birds at any function. I was just stepping out of the lift when the other elevator drew up and a frazzled Poonam bhabhi rushed out. Her hair was not completely set and her make-up was only half done. She admitted that she had pulled out the curlers and rushed down when informed that Amitabh and Jaya Bachchan had arrived. She dragged me to the banquet hall where the Bachchans had been seated. Amit-ji greeted me with a smile. I complimented him on the dashing purple shirt he was wearing, saying appreciatively, 'Sir, you are looking sexy.' He pointed out to me with typical Bachchanesque humour that he was seventy, and I repeated, 'Sir, you are looking sexy.' This time he turned to

Jaya-ji and complained with a twinkle in his eye, '*Dekho, kya keh raha hai yeh* Gulshan (Look at what Gulshan is saying).' Jaya-ji, who has always been affectionate towards me since my acting class days with Professor Roshan Taneja, responded with amusement. Relieved to see them smiling in my company, Poonam bhabhi went upstairs to hurry Kush and his bride, Taruna, to come down and receive their blessings.

I was chatting with Amit-ji and Jaya-ji when Shatru-ji entered with Rajinikanth Garu. Shatru-ji's voice boomed across the room, 'Amit, this is not a film shoot that you have to arrive so early.' Amit-ji responded to that good-natured jibe with one of his own. 'I didn't expect you to be on time, Sonu, but where is the bride and the groom? At least the children can be on time.' We all burst out laughing. Rajini Garu and I shared a great bond and when he saw me at the wedding, he told our host, 'I have found my friend Grover. You can leave me with him and go, Shatru-ji.' And thereafter we had a blast, like we had many times earlier when he had come to Mumbai on shoots and stayed over at my home.

One of my early encounters with Shatru-ji was on the sets of *Shiva Shakti*, directed by Govinda's uncle, Anand (Chitragupth) mama. The film featured Shatru-ji, Govinda, Anita Raj and Kimi Katkar in the lead, with me as the antagonist Junga Dada who wore his hair long, smoked a chillum and drove a jeep without ever using the brakes. My introduction scene had me toppling over vegetable carts and almost running down a child, till my crazy run is blocked by a truck owned by Shatru-ji. Blind with rage, I start smashing its windows with a rod while he watches from the window of a nearby dhaba. His character's quirk is that he won't interrupt his meal for anything or anyone. But after he is done, he steps out and takes me down with the first punch.

I found that illogical and reasoned with my action-director friend, Tinu Verma, who was a master of the game, that if we finished our fight in the very first scene, how would I, a feared goonda, keep the audience engaged till the climax? Tinu bhai pointed out to me that Shatru-ji had refused to take a beating from Vinod Khanna-ji in *Mere Apne* and had stormed out of the sets of *Kaala Patthar* when told that Amit-ji was going to give him a hiding with a 'belcha'. Why would he give in to the whims of a junior actor?

Unfazed, I marched up to Shatru-ji and told him that I needed to speak to him alone. He graciously sent everyone away and I repeated what I had told Tinu bhai. While others watched us from a distance and shook their heads over my foolish bravado, Shatru-ji heard me out quietly, and having started his career as a villain, saw the logic in what I was saying. He told Tinu bhai and Anand mama that he agreed with my point of view and appreciated my sincerity. He wanted the scene reworked, and it didn't matter if I got the better of him in that encounter because he would avenge himself in the end. Only a real 'hero' can take such decisions and Shatru-ji will always be mine. In the company of Shashi Ranjan, I have had many opportunities of hanging out socially with Shatru-ji, and each remains a cherished memory. He not only recommended me for many films, but when I confided in him about a long-cherished dream, he ensured it came true.

Those days, a film's mahurat shot was usually picturized on the hero and heroine or on two rival heroes. The first shot of *Seeta Salma Suzy* had been planned with the leading ladies Dimple Kapadia, Anita Raj and Salma Agha coming out in turns and speaking their lines with Shatru-ji finally emerging from the smoke to take the scene to its climax. 'Why me? Get Gulshan Grover to wind up the mahurat shot. The baddie anyway gets the better of everyone till the end,' he told the bemused director, Qamar Narvi. You can't argue with Shatru-ji and the director agreed but the heroines who were bigger names than me needed some convincing. Shatru-ji himself spoke to them and that's how

I got to be the big guy at the mahurat with Shatru-ji giving the ceremonial clap.

Even for *Gola Barood*, when David Dhawan informed him that the mahurat shot would feature Chunky Pandey and him, Shatru-ji insisted that it should have him and me. I got a frantic call from my friend and producer, Ravindra Dhanoa, urging me to rush to Hotel Horizon. No other baddie before me had featured in a mahurat shot. I will remain forever grateful to Shatru-ji for his support, his backing and blessings, thanks to which I added one more 'first' to my list and evolved as an actor.

7

FROM RUSSIA, WITH LOVE

Let's return to my struggling days for a moment. After *Ek Jaan Hai Hum*, the wonderful Mehras—F.C. Mehra, Parvesh C. Mehra, Rajiv Mehra and Umesh Mehra—probably impressed with my sincerity, hard work and simple nature, literally adopted me. I went on to do over twenty-five films with them for which I remain eternally grateful to them. One of them was a period romance based on a popular folklore. *Sohni Mahiwal* was an Indo-Russian co-production and Sunny Deol's first film outside his home banner, which he had signed even before his debut film *Betaab* released. It was directed by Umesh Mehra-ji and Latif Faiziyev, his Russian counterpart.

Sunny played Mirza Izzat Beg, who travels to India with his caravan in search of the girl of his dreams. He sees her in Sohni, the beautiful Poonam Dhillon, daughter of a poor potter, Tulla. I was cast as Noora who is determined to marry Sohni and will go to any lengths to separate Mirza and her. But the two continue to meet secretly till their love takes them to a watery end. One of my catchphrases, '*Ganna chus ke*', was a big hit with the audience.

It was a much talked-about project and there was a lot of opposition to my casting because many believed Noora should be played by someone taller and bigger, someone who was physically more threatening to Sunny. But Umesh-ji stood firm against the tide of 'nays'. He had immense faith in my talent and felt that my face worked for the character. He told his detractors to 'chill' and talk to him after the first schedule in Tashkent, confident that I would bring them around with my performance.

Sunny had trained for the action scenes while I had not received much training. Umesh-ji however supplied me with a lot of reading material and showed me other films in the genre at his theatre, Minerva. Being a Punjabi, I was familiar with the legend of Sohni–Mahiwal. Pran saab, who played Sohni's father Tulla, helped me during rehearsals, and to my delight, he announced that I was a good actor who didn't require much prep. That was high praise coming from an actor I had long admired. All through the shooting of the film, he continued to dole out welcome advice, and later even put in a good word for me to Harmesh Malhotra-ji for the Rishi Kapoor and Sridevi starrer *Banjaran* and several other producers in the south.

Chintu-ji, that wonderfully spontaneous actor who can give a perfect take even in his sleep, was taken aback during the shoot of *Banjaran* to see me tirelessly slog over my performance. Impressed with my commitment and always encouraging, he was among the first to recommend me to his producers and directors, telling them, 'Gulshan is very sincere, he will work hard even if his role is small.'

When I was cast as the lead in India's first mockumentary, *Bad Man*, by Viacom 18, in consultation with Group CEO Gaurav Gandhi (who has since moved to Amazon) and executive vice-president and head of creative Monika Shergill, we agreed that it would be great if we could get Chintu-ji to make a guest appearance in the film. I called and went across to meet him, hesitatingly requesting him to do this as a favour to me. He immediately agreed, 'My friend, it's done! Get the director and I will set things rolling.' Within a few minutes, I had arranged for Saumik Sen to discuss the project with him. A short while later, they called me to say that they would be shooting the next day at Mehboob Studio. What's more, Chintu-ji did not charge a rupee and wore his own clothes. Had it not been for these large-hearted actors, many of whom were my seniors and legends, I'm not sure I would have lasted in the film industry for so long.

Of course, my maddening dedication also exasperated a few people. Oscar-winning costume designer Bhanu Athaiya, who was in charge of the *Sohni Mahiwal*'s wardrobe, rang Umesh-ji one day to complain that his baddie would arrive at her workshop every day and sit with the tailors, requesting certain Punjabi-style buttons on a chain for his kurtas. 'I like his ideas, but I still want you to take Gulshan away from here,' Bhanu entreated. I was standing beside Umesh-ji and having heard every word she said, I was afraid he would throw me out. I was relieved when they both ended the conversation laughing over my 'commitment'.

When the costumes were ready, Bhanu invited me to Dharmendra-ji's Juhu bungalow for a fitting. I was afraid that if Paaji saw me in my costume and thought I didn't 'look' like Noora, he might want me dropped. So, I told Bhanu that I would swing by her workshop instead. She wouldn't hear of it, telling me I didn't have to drive all the way to 'town' when she was going to be in the suburbs with Sunny's costumes. With no excuses left, I sneaked into Paaji's bungalow at the appointed time, praying that no one would see me and exclaim, 'Yeh villain hai!' I ducked into an empty room, quickly tried on my clothes and ran away before I could be spotted.

Soon after that, we went behind the Iron Curtain for the film's first schedule. We were put up at the best five-star hotel in Tashkent. Every celebrity from India had stayed there, including Raj Kapoor saab. On the day we arrived, I was invited to a meet-and-greet session with the team, particularly our Russian counterparts, many of whom we were meeting for the first time. All of us, including Umesh-ji and his wife Ritu bhabhi, my co-stars Sunny, Zeenat Aman-ji and Rakesh Bedi and our cinematographer S. Pappu, had gathered in the restaurant below. After a warm welcome from the local cast and crew, we got down to learning about them and their beautiful country, which had earlier embraced Raj saab's tramp in *Awara* and Mithun-da's *Disco Dancer*.

As Noora, I was sporting long hair, a beard and a burnished tan for which I had to sit in the burning sun for hours. To top it off, my eyes were streaked with soorma. I looked like a cross between an Italian hero, a la *Sandokan*, and a Punjabi baddie. My distinctive look set me apart. After a while, the waiter approached our table with a bottle of vodka, informing me in broken English that a lady sitting across the room had sent it over with her compliments. I was left red-faced by the unexpected attention. While everyone laughed at my heightened colour, I simply nodded and accepted the bottle while avoiding the eyes of my admirer.

Fifteen minutes later, the lady sent me a local dish through the same waiter, who, this time around, informed that 'she like you'. Awkwardly, I tried to wave away the gift, but Zeenat-ji, who was sitting beside me, reprimanded me, saying that was no way to treat a lady. She insisted that I thank her personally. By now I had realized that my Russian fan was a big shot because only someone really wealthy and well connected would be allowed to enter that restaurant. This added to my discomfort. Despite my obvious reluctance, Zeenat-ji took my hand and led me to the lady's table, giving me a gentle push in her direction. I mumbled a thank you, still avoiding eye contact, conscious that everyone in the room was looking at us. Meanwhile, my besotted admirer was going crazy, making my sceptical team realize that Russian women found me extremely attractive. And that's how, on the first day of the schedule, from a not-wanted Noora I became the noor (gem) of the film!

Zeenat-ji played the dangerous dacoit Zarina, who lived in a large camp filled with tents and horses. It was a daringly different role for her, but Umesh-ji, who was a good friend and lived in the same building as she did, Bakhtawar, had been able to persuade her to do the film. Noora approaches Zarina for help after he fails to stop Sohni from meeting Mirza, knowing she has an axe to grind with the family. Zeenat-ji is a diva and a delight to work with.

The Russians were a talented lot and gracious in their hospitality. The local interpreters, who had learnt the language formally, spoke better Hindi than many of us Indians. So, instead of saying, '*Aap khana kha lijiye, phir gaadi aapko location le jayega* (Please have your lunch, then the car will take you to the film's location),' they would say, '*Aap dopahar ka bhojan kar lijeye, uske baad aapka vahan apko cinema bhoomi tak le jayegi*.' I had learnt certain Russian words before leaving India, so I could communicate with the locals and find my way around town. Things were going smoothly until a mishap happened.

I had taken several lessons in sword fighting for a confrontation scene with Mirza from Tinu Verma at a ground in Amboli before we left Mumbai. The swords provided were not the cardboard variety we were given back home; these ones were sharp. While fencing with him, I inadvertently sliced through Sunny's thumb and he started bleeding profusely. Distraught, I stammered my apologies. Sunny was very understanding, pointing out that such accidents happened during a shoot, but others on the set were not quite so sympathetic. He was rushed to a hospital to stem the flow of blood and the shooting ground to an abrupt halt.

In Russia they have strict rules. A doctor won't release a patient from hospital till completely satisfied that he or she is out of danger. The injury was deep. Since Sunny had lost a lot of blood, he had been given a tetanus shot and antibiotics, and they thought it prudent for him to spend a few days on a hospital bed with his hand bandaged. He tried convincing the doctors that he was fine, but they were deaf to his pleas. As a result, the film's schedule was delayed, and the blame automatically fell on me. This cast a cloud over the shoot and I feared they might send me back and replace me with another actor. However, Umesh-ji, Latif Faiziyev and Sunny were all convinced it was an accident, and so I stayed on.

Back home, we continued filming in Mumbai's Chandivali Studio with the climax picturized in excavated caves on the outskirts of Delhi. We also shot in Chandigarh where many beautiful girls turned up on the sets and, without a second glance at me, headed straight for Sunny with their autograph books. Fresh from my conquests in Russia, I thought they had overlooked me because I was unrecognizable in a turban and beard. So, I requested Ritu bhabhi and Poonam to shout, 'O Gulshan, Gulshan Grover . . .' when I strolled past them with carefully cultivated nonchalance. I thought this would alert the girls of my presence, but to my shock, as soon as my identity was revealed, they ran for the exit. That was the terror I had unleashed with *Sadma*, *Avtaar* and *Mashaal*!

Sohni Mahiwal released in Russia six months after its India release. The film put me in the bracket of the ace villains of the time, and thanks to Umesh-ji and the trust he reposed in me, I shone bright. People came out of theatres raving about my performance and hating Noora. I also owed my success partly to Bhanu Athaiya, to the film's action directors Pappu and Tinu Verma, the guidance of Pran saab, the magnanimity of Sunny and Zeenat Aman-ji, as also Poonam and Rakesh Bedi's constant support. The film's director of photography, Pappu Sheikh, along with his Russian counterparts, Davron Abdullayev, Abdul Rashid Papu and Abduliev Duran, lit me up beautifully onscreen.

After the film's screening, Dharmendra Paaji hugged me and praised me profusely. And to think I was once worried that he would have me replaced. Years later, when we were working

together in a film directed by K.C. Bokadia-ji, the action director
had conceived a scene that had me picking up Paaji and throwing
him to the ground. Bokadia-ji shook his head disapprovingly and
told the action director, 'No, no, he's "He-man" Dharmendra,
Gulshan Grover can't do that to him!' Paaji smiled and told
him graciously, 'It's okay, Bokadia-ji, he's like my son,' but the
producer–director argued that if the scene was played out this
way, people wouldn't watch the film. We finally arrived at a
compromise: I was to push Paaji to the ground, but not bodily lift
him over my head and hurl him down.

Zeenat-ji was equally generous with her compliments. She
later recommended me for a Rajinikanth starrer. Those days a
south Indian film was a big deal because we got paid in cash,
sometimes on the first day of the shoot itself, and I was thrilled.
Unfortunately, I couldn't do the film because the dates clashed
with another film I was working on. But Zeenat-ji still remains
one of the many from my fraternity who gave me wings in this
flight to stardom and I will remain indebted to the Mehras for
helping me soar.

8

IN TORONTO, WITH THE UNDERTAKER

Sohni Mahiwal's success and my growing popularity as an actor gave me the creative liberty to collaborate with many of my directors in creating a character after a story narration. The responsibility initially took me by surprise, and I wasn't sure if I was up to the task. But slowly, I began to enjoy the process. For one such film, I had planned several different get-ups and was eager to discuss clothes and accessories with Umesh Mehra-ji who was directing it. But he was busy with other things and kept putting me off whenever I called him. Impatient to run my 'look' by him, I contemplated getting myself photographed. But hiring a good photographer was expensive and I couldn't expect my friend Nath Gupta to keep doing shoots with me for free. So, there was just one thing left to do.

Umesh-ji had told me that he was home till eight in the morning, after which we could meet at his office. But he had also confided that he would be going out of town shortly to scout for locations. One morning, I turned up at his doorstep without any warning. Ritu bhabhi opened the door and screamed out loud. Her cry brought Umesh-ji hurrying across and for a minute even he was stumped. Finally, he recognized me in my get-up and burst out laughing, very appreciative of my effort. Now, vastly amused, Ritu bhabhi called her in-laws, who lived in another building in the same compound, as also Umesh-ji's brother, Rajiv, and his wife, Mita, urging them to come over. They came running and, to my delight, gave my 'look' a collective thumbs up.

The film for which I had taken such pains for was titled *Kasam* and had Anil Kapoor as an undercover cop who goes to a village to catch drug peddlers in action. There he falls in love with Poonam Dhillon, the daughter of the village headman, played by Pran saab, who in a blotched-up operation, ends up crippled and embittered. I take over from him as the new headman, Jinda, to continue with the fight.

After seeing me in my 'costume', Umesh-ji assured me that the role of Jinda was mine and that I would get a call soon confirming the offer from his producers, Indra Kumar (fondly called Indu) and Ashok Thakeria. Umesh-ji had warned me that it was a challenging part and would require a lot of my time. I was ready for the challenge.

Excited about *Kasam*, Umesh-ji and I were on the phone almost every day discussing the film and my character. He would keep asking me if Indu or Ashok had called, and I would reply in the negative. Then, one day, when he had a meeting with them, Indu confided to Umesh-ji that his sister, actress Aruna Irani-ji, had suggested Danny Denzongpa-ji for the role of Jinda. Tutu, who was present at the meeting, told me years later what had transpired in the room. Umesh-ji heard Indu out quietly, then, closing the script, got to his feet, saying, 'If you can't understand why I want someone specific for a role, I suggest you make the film without me.' The next day, the long-awaited call came. I don't blame Indu. Aruna-ji was an industry veteran and as her brother, he couldn't just dismiss her suggestion. But he also understood that his director had something in mind which is why he was insisting on me, and being a director himself, he surrendered to Umesh-ji's vision. *Kasam* remains one of my most memorable films, as much for the role as the confidence these film-makers had in me.

I went on to do several films with Umesh-ji, including three from the *Khiladi* series—*Sabse Bada Khiladi, Khiladiyon Ka Khiladi* and *International Khiladi*—which gave my brother and constant support Akshay Kumar the adage of 'Khiladi Kumar'. I have fond memories of *Khiladiyon Ka Khiladi* which pitted me against Rekha-ji and former WWE wrestlers 'Crush' and 'The Undertaker'. The film—the fourth in the franchise—had Rekha-ji playing a don, Maya, who hosts illegal wrestling matches in New York with the support of the local police commissioner. My character, King Don, was full of swagger. He was always dressed in a long coat, which concealed the fact that half his hand was missing. One of my dialogues became a constant refrain with the audience, '*Maya, tera to mein palat doonga kaya.*'

A week before we started shooting in Toronto, I introduced Rekha-ji to Deepa Mehta, a wonderful director and a good friend. She wanted Rekha-ji to play the role of the elder sister-in-law, Radha, in her Indo-Canadian drama *Fire*. The talks, however, fell through because Rekha-ji, I believe, had certain inhibitions, finding the role too bold, given the lesbian eroticism inherent in it. Shabana Azmi-ji eventually took up the role.

Rekha-ji and I continued to share a fantastic working relationship through the making of *Khiladiyon Ka Khiladi*. We had some major confrontation scenes, in which I was supposed to get really nasty and disrespectful towards her. They made me nervous till Rekha-ji pointed out that I should be true to my character without worrying about offending and upsetting her. She is extremely professional and a true diva!

We had worked together in Mohan Segal-ji's *Kasam Suhaag Ki*. Segal-ji, her mentor-director, was on a comeback trail. The revenge drama was driven by Rekha-ji, with me playing Thakur Yuvraj Singh. Between shots, Rekha-ji, a talented artist, would sketch out different looks for me to experiment with. She is ethereally beautiful. To describe her, I will borrow a phrase from Shakespeare's play *Antony and Cleopatra*: 'Age cannot wither her nor custom stale her infinite variety.' She's our Indian Cleopatra who keeps fit through yoga, whereas Akshay Kumar who is still the fittest actor in the industry today and a role model for many, sets up his own akhada wherever he goes. So, we had two physical fitness experts and enthusiastic trainers in Toronto. Between Madam Rekha and Mr Khiladi, I never missed my morning jog and exercises with these two.

The presence of the WWE wrestlers, particularly The Undertaker—a true in-ring pioneer with many titles under his belt—added to the excitement of being a part of the hit franchise. He looked mysterious with his face covered and at the same time dangerous too during the televised wrestling matches and we all wondered what The Undertaker was like for real, waiting eagerly for him to arrive. We had only seen him on TV till then, his face shielded by his long hair and his brooding silences punctuated by his fists of fury. When we finally saw him in person, everyone, including Akshay, who, in the film, finally gets the better of this six-foot-ten-inch giant weighing 140 kg, was intimidated by his persona.

The Undertaker drove to the set straight from the airport, and without a single word of greeting, simply stood there, scanning Akshay from head to toe. After taking his measure, the WWE wrestler glared at our Khiladi and growled menacingly, 'So, you are the one?' Before Akshay could react, he pivoted on his heel and asked to be escorted to his make-up room. We all stood there transfixed, watching him walk away.

Later, when the line producer was figuring out with Jodi Lynn, The Undertaker's petite wife, manager and make-up woman, what to get him for lunch, the late Keshu Ramsay, our producer and a fantastic host, magnanimously instructed them to bring two of every dish so that the food wouldn't fall short. The Undertaker turned from the mirror and roared, 'Get ten of each!'

The next day, he headed straight for Keshu's wife, a sweet lady, and snarled, 'And you, you better watch out too!' Her eyes were wide with shock and fear. Every day, The Undertaker would target someone, leaving us wondering if we had done something to upset the big man and if he would really carry out his threat.

Even though we were adversaries onscreen, in real life Akshay and I are like brothers, constantly together. Between shots, I would duck into his car parked just outside the location and we would chat or listen to music. One day, as we sat together, we felt the earth begin to shake and our car swung violently from left to right. Terrified, we looked out of the window fearing an earthquake only to find that the rest of the cars in the parking lot were still grounded. Perplexed, we turned around and spotted The Undertaker with our car in his hands like a toy, swinging it like a pendulum. He took care not to damage the SUV or hurt us, but he still managed to make our blood turn cold. As soon as he put the car down, we jumped out and scurried away, his guffaws following us all the way back to the set.

Weeks later, Neelam, the local line producer, admitted that The Undertaker had been playing pranks on us. To our surprise, we also found that his wife Jodi would do Crush's make-up as well. The two WWE wrestlers, whom we had seen baying for each other's blood on television, were very considerate towards each other off camera. Their camaraderie was like the bonding Akshay and I shared. In fact, after shooting with him, even The Undertaker was impressed with Akshay's agility in their action scenes together.

Akshay and I went on to do three more *Khiladi* films together, for which he recommended me strongly for the villain's role, and each one was a blast. My Punjabi pra's mental make-up is such that he is never late. He would often come knocking on my hotel door at an ungodly hour. If he found me still in the shower or getting dressed, he would make my life hell. '*Chal na yaar*, you don't have to bathe for so long and you can always tie your shoelaces in the car. Now hurry, I don't want to be late,' he would nag me. I would affectionately point out that I still had a few minutes before I had to leave and he should go ahead, but my words would fall on deaf ears as he would drag me out of my room and into his car. Early call time also meant I couldn't stay out late. Akshay Kumar drilled the importance of punctuality in me and ensured that we invariably reached the sets on time. He continues to be as punctual as ever—even today when we are shooting for Rohit Shetty's *Sooryavanshi*. We've had our creative disagreements, but they never blew up into anything nasty because there was always Umesh-ji to play referee. To this day he remains my dearest friend.

Except for one Saif Ali Khan starrer, *Aashik Aawara*, I featured in almost all of Umesh-ji's films. He had also signed me for *Aashik Aawara*, but a couple of days before we were to roll, there arose a problem. I had a shoot on the same dates with another producer. Even though I did everything possible to get those dates released from the other producer so I could work with my mentor, I failed. Umesh-ji was upset, but there was no way he could delay his shoot. So, he let me go, saying brusquely, 'Go along, I don't want you.' Since I had experienced his soda bottle-kind of anger before, I knew it would fizzle out soon.

We reunited a year later for *Sabse Bada Khiladi*, in which I played the cunning Kekada, followed by King Don in *Khiladiyon Ka Khiladi*, the landlord Mangal Singh in *Qila*, Thakral in *International Khiladi*, and Gullu in *Yeh Mohabbat Hai*. And the 'bad man' continued to make a good impression onscreen more so when he had Mr Khiladi, Akshay Kumar, for company. I will always be indebted to him for the emotional person he is. I can never forget how when we met on the first day of the *Sooryavanshi* shoot, and even after all these years, his first question to me was: 'How is your son Sanjay doing in Hollywood?'

9

A NEW AVTAAR

In my struggling days, I would often visit Mahesh Bhatt saab's Pali Hill home. Bhatt saab was always warm and welcoming, and one day, offered me a role in *Arth*.

Arth was a semi-autobiographical drama which revolved around Pooja, a homemaker, her film-maker husband Inder Malhotra, and Kavita Sanyal, the schizophrenic movie star with whom Inder has an affair. What made it a path-breaking film was that having found her purpose in life, Pooja was able to turn away not just her husband when he sought a reconciliation, but even her singer-friend who wanted to marry her. I was grateful to have bagged a role in this film when I was still struggling for a foothold in the industry. But in my greed for publicity, I almost got thrown out of the film.

Back then, strugglers didn't get invited to film parties or featured in popular film magazines like *Filmfare*, *Cine Blitz*, *Stardust* or a prestigious trade weekly like *Screen*. The only way to find a mention in these magazines was to drop by their offices and meet the editors. Rita Mehta, the editor of *Cine Blitz*, agreed to carry my interview provided I spoke about *Arth*. There were speculations in the press that the film was based on Bhatt saab and Parveen Babi-ji's extramarital affair, but the film-makers were neither confirming nor denying these rumours, making the gossip mills churn overtime. In return for the promised write-up, I admitted to Rita that Smita-ji's character, Kavita, was indeed modelled on Parveen-ji, the troubled Bollywood actress, while Shabana-ji's character, Pooja, was inspired partly by Bhatt saab's wife, Kiran-ji. Kulbhushan Kharbanda, who played the 'hero' Inder, found his muse in Bhatt saab himself. My character, Gulshan, was borrowed from Parveen-ji's manager, Ved Sharma.

Rita was delighted with the scoop and my photograph appeared alongside Smita-ji and Shabana-ji in the spread. Since the story was attributed to a 'source', I had presumed, somewhat naively, that no one would suspect me, not realizing that my photograph appearing alongside the two leading ladies was an immediate giveaway.

Soon after the article appeared, Bhatt saab summoned me to his home. He asked me if I was responsible for the news break. I tried to bluff my way out, but he is an astute man and told me gently, 'Beta, I know you have done this. The producer (Kuljit Pal) is very upset about all this leaking out. I justified your actions by pointing out that you are a newcomer who wanted to give an interview.' I confessed to him then and was really worried that I would get the boot, but Bhatt saab assured me that he would sort out the issue with the producer. Thanks to his intervention, I remained in the film, and for this I will always remain grateful to him.

Rita Mehta and I went on to become friends and she published many of my interviews. She even recommended my name for the 'Giants' Award in Art and Cinema, which I bagged in 2003.

After this incident, Bhatt saab became my mentor and guide. I would often drop by his Bandra home, and years later his Juhu home and office, to chat with him. The first person I usually bumped into as soon as I entered his apartment building was his daughter Pooja. There were several other regulars upstairs, from

Anupam Kher (with whom I always enjoyed working in later years and who is like a brother and a close friend, a relationship I can never find words to describe, except to say that I always feel he has more affection for Anil Kapoor than for me) and Dalip Tahil to Shabana-ji, Smita-ji, Kulbhushan Kharbanda and Raj Kiran (who played the ghazal singer and Pooja's friend in *Arth*). Bhatt saab was always encouraging, full of positivity, but his affection did not translate into any more roles. In fact, after *Hum Paanch* and *Rocky*, I wasn't getting much work and it was only my teaching job at Professor Roshan Taneja saab's acting school that kept me going.

Frustration was beginning to corrode my self-confidence when late one evening, I stopped by Vinay Shukla-ji's Santa Cruz residence. He was the writer of *Hum Paanch*, and having worked together, I knew him well. Vinay-ji's wife, Neelam bhabhi, had an unspoken rule that if you turned up when they were sitting down for a meal, you had to eat with them. I would time my visits in such a way that, occasionally, I could enjoy a home-cooked meal. I was, however, careful not to turn up too frequently and lose their respect.

It was customary for everyone to take their shoes off before entering Vinay-ji's apartment. That evening Shabana-ji was with him. She knew me well because I would often drop by her Janki Kutir residence or on her set, accompanied by Anil Kapoor, to ask for advice and hope for recommendations and introductions. She pointedly looked at my feet, particularly my socks that had multiple holes in them, and asked with the familiarity of a well-wisher, 'Why are you wearing torn socks, Gulshan?'

Burning with embarrassment and frustration, I told her that my situation was as miserable as my socks.

'What do you mean?' she prodded, and I admitted that I had no work and consequently, little money for even the essentials.

'Do you have any photographs in stock?' she enquired gently, and I replied eagerly that I had plenty.

'Not the ones where you look like a goonda, brandishing a dagger or wielding a stick. Get some decent ones and come to my place tomorrow,' she instructed.

My spirits lifted instantly and quickly excusing myself, I dashed straight to my photographer friend, Nath Gupta, and told him that Shabana-ji wanted some 'decent' pictures and that I didn't have any. Nath Gupta, bless his soul, agreed to a photo shoot. I was happy, knowing he wouldn't charge me.

I was up at dawn and he clicked some beautiful pictures of me just as the sun came up. I followed him back to his studio, waiting impatiently while he developed and printed them. As soon as the photographs were dry, I rushed with them to Shabana-ji's house. She also requested her brother, director of photography Baba Azmi, to shoot some pictures of me. Baba and his assistant, Thomas Xavier, clicked some more photographs and she gave all of them to Mohan Kumar-ji to convince him to let me play the role of her son in the family drama *Avtaar*, which had Rajesh Khanna-ji as her husband.

The children of film stars usually inherit the good looks of their parents, which cuts actors like me out of the picture. Fortunately for me, Mohan Kumar-ji was scouting for a boy who looked ordinary but was ambitious. By casting me in his film, he was going against the grain. But he thought I was the perfect fit for the role of a henpecked husband of a rich man's spoilt daughter, who leaves his parents' modest home at the drop of a hat to join his father-in-law's business.

On the set, the always benevolent Shabana-ji took it upon herself to not just mentor me, but like a fairy godmother, she also guided me on social niceties. She would nudge me to wish Kaka-ji when he drove in, then point me in the direction of the make-up room to learn my lines. Once I knew them well, I would rehearse my scenes with her before facing the camera.

Avtaar was released on 11 March 1983, and excited to see me sharing the frame with superstars like Rajesh Khanna-ji and Shabana Azmi-ji, my erstwhile neighbours, friends and family flocked to the theatres in groups of fifteen to twenty. They returned home disappointed, complaining to Pitaji and Chaiji that their sanskari, soft-spoken son who had stood first class first in high school and gone to the gurudwara every morning, was no longer the same Gulshan.

Even though I now lived miles away, they believed that my bond with my family was as strong as ever and were horrified to discover that I had become selfish and materialistic, abandoning my parents for a better life. '*Munda bigad gaya hai*,' they sighed, shaking their heads despondently. My mother and sisters tried to explain to them that what they had seen in the film was make-believe. 'He still goes to the gurudwara every morning. He's still the same Gulshan,' they insisted, but the neighbours weren't convinced. That was a big high for me. My portrayal had literally hit home.

Professionally, *Avtaar* changed my career's direction. The film was a big hit and I came to be perceived by industry veterans as an actor with a distinctive look, acting style and dialogue delivery. It brought along a flood of offers, and with the success of *Sohni Mahiwal*, I was finally an actor on the rise. As I flitted from one studio to the next, making a name and carving a niche for myself as a baddie with films like *Ram Lakhan*, *Saudagar* and *Umar 55 Ki Dil Bachpan Ka*, Bhatt saab and I drifted apart because of our respective commitments.

He surprised me with a call one morning, asking me where I was. When I told him I was filming, Bhatt saab instructed me to hop across to Filmalaya Studio. I didn't think twice. I was shooting for Raj N. Sippy's *Amaanat* and I went in my costume during lunch break. He offered me a role in his upcoming film *Sir*, which was about two ganglords, a teacher and his young students. He told me that although it wasn't a big part, it was definitely an interesting one. He thought I could play the role convincingly. He wanted me to play the demented, dangerous younger brother of the film's main villain. I was a big star by then, but I immediately accepted the offer because it had come from my mentor Mahesh Bhatt saab.

A couple of days before *Sir* was to go on the floor, I wanted some date adjustments and mentioned the film to the producer I was shooting with. Sadashiv Amrapurkar bhai who was playing the main villain of *Sir* was in the vicinity and overheard me. He hurried across to Bhatt saab, arguing that in an ensemble cast of 'serious' performers like Naseeruddin Shah, Paresh Rawal and Pooja Bhatt, a 'commercial' actor like me would stand out like a sore thumb. Sadashiv bhai was a phenomenally talented actor but Bhatt saab was anything but prejudiced. He was incensed by the insinuation that I was not on par with the rest of the cast and told his brother Mukesh Bhatt-ji, who was producing the film, that he wanted to replace Sadashiv bhai. He wondered if his decision would create any problems with the distributors because Sadashiv bhai's portrayal of the eunuch, Maharani, in Bhatt saab's blockbuster *Sadak*, had made him a saleable name. Mukesh-ji, who never cowed down to market dictates, told Bhatt saab that he could work with whoever he wanted.

Unaware of what was happening behind the scenes, I got myself photographed wearing my son Sanjay's bermudas and took the pictures to Bhatt saab to ask him if the 'boy-man' look worked for the character. He waved them off and to my delight told me that I would now be playing Jimmy, the main villain, and we would start shooting the day after. I was on cloud nine but requested at least four days of prep. Mukesh-ji wasn't happy to hear this because the set at Mukesh Mills was ready and any delay would cost money, but Bhatt saab assured me that they would wait. The character I was to play earlier was turned into a woman, Sweety, and Sushmita Mukherjee was signed for it.

During a two-hour briefing, Bhatt saab explained that Jimmy wasn't a regular gangster; he was the anti-hero who wanted to avenge the death of his younger sibling who had been stripped and hanged by Veljibhai, a rival don played by Paresh. His plan was to do the same with Veljibhai's innocent teenage daughter, Pooja. As a result of this threat, Pooja was placed under house arrest. Naseer, who was her 'Sir', tries to engineer a truce between the two dons only to realize that he was jeopardizing his own life in the process.

While prepping for my character and working on his emotional graph, I got a photo shoot done by Pradeep Chandra, my old friend and a *Times of India* photographer, this time wearing my own designer suits. I also got my make-up man, Suresh Sharma Dada, to cosmetically put a hundred pockmarks on my face, convinced that this would make the character look distinctive. I imitated Bhatt saab's gesture of whipping off his glasses whenever he wanted to underline a point and was soon living the role of Jimmy who was rechristened Chhappan Tikli after the first few shots.

I remember one scene where I rage at my six-foot-plus henchman for losing a fight to the rival camp, randomly firing bullets in the air. I drew Bhatt saab's attention to the fact that I had done similar scenes in other films before and requested him if we could figure out something different. The genius that he is, Bhatt saab came up with an idea that took me back to my acting school days. He outlined a scenario, like Professor Roshan Taneja saab used to for our 'improvisation' sessions and told me to imagine that I was a director whose 'hero' had not yet shown up on the set while, oblivious to his anger and frustration, his assistants are happily enjoying their lunch, even wondering what is for dessert.

My parents, to whose sacrifices I owe everything in life

With Deepak Khetrapal, Simrit Kaur (principal, Shri Ram College of Commerce, Delhi) and Justice Arjan Kumar Sikri

With Arun Jaitley

With Sunil Sethi

With Shri L.K. Advani
and Pratibha Advani

With Karisma Kapoor,
Meenakshi Seshadri
and Pooja Bhatt

With playback
singer Shabbir
Kumar and
Mithun
Chakraborty

With K.C. Bokadia
and Rajinikanth

With Kamal Haasan and director Balu Mahendra, with whom I made
the memorable *Sadma*

With Yash Chopra and Rishi Kapoor on the sets of *Vijay*

With Smita Patil and Kulbhushan Kharbanda, on the sets of *Arth*

With Shabana Azmi

Bonding over a glass of juice

Sanjay, with his mother Philomina Lobo

With my son, Sanjay

Sanjay with Ajay Sethi and the CEO of Media Zone, Abu Dhabi

Sanjay with Tiger Shroff and Hollywood producer Larry Kasanoff

With Aamir Khan

With Akshay Kumar, The Undertaker and Umesh Mehra

With the superstars of superstars, Amitabh Bachchan and Rajinikanth

With one of my mentors, Mahesh Bhatt-ji, and his talented daughter Pooja

With Dilip Kumar-ji on the sets of *Mashaal*

With Sunil Dutt saab, who produced one of my first films, *Rocky*

With my acting guru, Professor Roshan Taneja

With my close friend Shashi Ranjan, and the iconic Chintu-ji, one of the most
spontaneous actors I have come across

With Om Puri and Naseeruddin Shah on the sets of *Shoot On Sight*

With Jeetendra-ji and Sanjay Dutt

Receiving the best actor award at the San Francisco film festival for the film *Badman*

With T-Series honcho Bhushan Kumar and ace director Sanjay Gupta

With Bipin Patel and Rani Mukerji, lighting up the Empire State Building on India Day

With Carnival Group Chairman Shrikant Bhasi and P.V.S. Sunil (MD)

With Ash Gupta, who always stood rock solid by me while I chased my
Hollywood dream

With Navin Luther, Jackie Shroff and Navin's daughter Dibya

With Manisha Koirala, Abhinav Chaturvedi and Vivek Mushran on
the sets of *Saudagar*

On the sets of the Polish film, *Nie Means Nie*

With two of my closest buddies, Suniel Shetty and Mahima Chaudhry

With Tina Ambani, one of my closest friends in the film industry

With Shah Rukh Khan, international show organizer Farhath Hussain
and Aamir Khan

With Shatrughan Sinha-ji and the gutsy producer Pahlaj Nihalani

What an experience to be in the presence of His Holiness the Dalai Lama

With Prince Charles

With Ashok Amritraj and Jean-Claude Van Damme

With the legendary Al Pacino

With Duncan McLachlan, the director of *The Second Jungle Book: Mowgli & Baloo*, which put me on the Hollywood map

With Steven Seagal

With Arnold Schwarzenegger

With Salma Hayek

With Goldie Hawn

With Steven Spielberg

With Janet Hirshenson and Jane Jenkins, casting directors of the James Bond film, *Casino Royale*

With Mahesh Bhatt

With Rohit Shetty and Akshay Kumar on the sets of my forthcoming film, *Sooryavanshi*

Bhatt saab ordered the most expensive items on the menu from a nearby hotel and warned me not to share what was to happen with anyone in the cast or crew. On camera, the actors playing my henchmen were happily tucking in when I suddenly jumped to my feet and, violently overturning the table, raged, 'How can you eat after such a failure?' The shock and fear on their faces was for real, as was my anger. The scene, to borrow the title of a Hollywood film, made a 'sudden impact' even with the audience!

Another scene that impressed even Naseer is when his character proposes a truce between Chhappan Tikli and Veljibhai. I hear him out silently, before replying, 'Have you thought how after saying this to me you are going to get out of here alive?' The line was pronounced without heat, and despite the fact that I made no threats, it reeked of quiet menace.

With Bhatt saab guiding me, I came out of *Sir* with flying colours, winning some awards along the way and plenty of accolades. After this, we worked on many films together, including *Tadipaar*, *Naaraaz*, *Criminal*, *Duplicate* and *Angaaray*.

Naaraaz was the first Hindi film to be shot in Malaysia and the first shot had me walking around with Mithun-da's character. He saves my life from an assassin and I tell him how I had come to the country as a penniless youth and am now a wealthy gangster with a beautiful moll, played by Soni Razdan, who loves me for the money and power I have amassed. I had to pull off a sixty-line monologue in a single take. I was ready and waiting for the challenge when Bhatt saab arrived, telling me jokingly to ask him all the questions that were on my mind before he got too busy. He then looked around for Soni and when told that she was finishing her make-up, threatened to throw his wife out of the film if she didn't arrive pronto. Soni turned up soon after, as did Mithun-da, and the shot went off smoothly.

However, as is my habit, as soon as Bhatt saab shouted, 'Cut', I ran to him saying, 'One more, sir.' Like Anil Kapoor and Aamir Khan, I am never happy with the first shot, always believing I can improve. Mithun-da, who had given me my first lessons in acting and had always been affectionate towards me, walked up to Mukesh-ji, who had joined us, and quipped tongue-in-cheek, 'With this "One More" around we will be doing this scene for the next twenty days and the schedule will be over before you know it.' In my enthusiasm to coax Bhatt saab for a retake, I told him to shut up. Despite being older than me and a more popular star, Mithun-da graciously allowed me to shut him up that day. But he didn't forget the incident.

A few days later, Bhatt saab was filming an action scene that required me to shoot at Mithun-da from a helicopter. Back then, there were no cell phones and walkie-talkies, so I had strict instructions to stand outside the hotel in my costume at 4 p.m. for the car that would drive me to the helipad. Dressed in my black suit, trench coat and dark glasses, I was there right on time. Just then, a group of foreigners drove up. One of them shouted out to me, 'Bellboy, get our bags.' I was shocked that a star like me was being called 'bellboy'. I was looking around, wondering if anyone had been a witness to my insult, when I spotted Mithun-da and Avtar Gill laughing their guts out. I guessed that they had told these foreigners that I was the bellboy. I ran after them, abusing them loudly, as the pranksters dashed into the lobby of the hotel.

Bhatt saab, who had packed up early but had no way of informing me of the change of plans, arrived just then, and hearing the commotion, hurried after me wondering what had set me off. Spying Avtar and a guffawing Mithun-da who was trying to rile me up further, shouting, 'Hey boy, bring up my bags too,' he guessed what had happened and joined in the laughter. Mithun-da is the president of the prankster's club, along with Ajay Devgn, Suniel Shetty, Sanjay Dutt, Raza Murad and late entrant Amitabh

Bachchan-ji as its members, with Avtar Gill is its secretary. Those were such fun times!

Impressed with my dedication, Bhatt saab would sing my praises to journalists, introduce me to people who mattered, and when he spotted me at parties looking nervous and awkward, he would beckon me over and keep me around him. On set, he even acted out scenes and would work on the character with me. Occasionally, he would also tease me, saying, 'Pooja, take Gulshan away, I'm not ready for his sincerity, it scares me. He will ask me a hundred questions for which I am not prepared yet. Let me read the scene first before you let him loose on me.' His words, spoken in jest, made us all laugh, but my sincerity left a lasting impression on his daughter and my buddy Pooja.

Malaysia was sweltering, and one day on the sets of *Naaraaz*, Mithun-da, Atul Agnihotri and Pooja were hollering at the assistant director for getting them out of their air-conditioned rooms too early. Mithun-da was wearing shorts, Atul was dressed in lightweight trousers and a shirt, while Pooja looked pretty in a summery dress. All three were complaining about the heat, when Pooja suddenly spotted me sitting like a stoic Buddha in a corner. I was bundled up in a black suit and tie, with a trench coat on top. My face was caked with make-up and criss-crossed with hundreds of cuts dressed up with chemicals that burned in the heat. Fish skin was stuck to my eyes to make them look small, give me an 'Oriental' look, and my hair was gelled back with an egg-white mask. Despite the obvious discomfort, I did not complain even once. One look at me and Pooja calmed down instantly. She later told me that in that moment, faced with my sincerity, all her anger melted away. 'This incident is going into my autobiography when I write one,' she promised.

I gave some of my best performances in Bhatt saab's films too, right up to *Zakhm*. Produced by Mukesh-ji for Pooja Bhatt Productions, *Zakhm*, written and directed by Bhatt saab, was based on his own strained relationship with his film-maker father, Nanabhai Bhatt. It bagged child actor Kunal Khemu and leading man Ajay Devgn National Awards. I was given the role of a Sardarji, Gurdayal Singh. I had allotted the 7 a.m. to 2 p.m. slot to Priyadarshan for the climax of his film *Hera Pheri* in which I played the kidnapper Kabeera but had assured Mukesh-ji that I would be with them after that. Then, the unexpected happened.

When Priyadarshan arrived on the set, he discovered that a shaft of sunlight he wanted streaming in through the skylight to light up the frame would only be possible to capture after noon. This meant that my scenes could only be shot later in the day. 'But I have to leave by 1.30 p.m. at the latest,' I wailed. Priyadarshan was apologetic but firm, saying the earliest he could take the shot was 1 p.m.

It was a big set and the entire cast of *Hera Pheri* and over a hundred fighters had been hired for the day, along with props. I couldn't leave them high and dry. Firoz Nadiadwala, a successful and influential producer, spoke to Bhatt saab and explained things to him. He was upset and told me brusquely, 'Go, shoot your film, I will get someone else for the role.' I understood the emotion underlying his words and it broke my heart. Saurabh Shukla eventually played the role and I will always rue the fact that I didn't get to work in the iconic film.

My innings with the Bhatts hadn't yet ended. For her film *Jism*, Pooja was looking for someone to play Bipasha Basu's millionaire husband, Rohit Khanna. I was later told that they had some big heroes in mind. But Bhatt saab pointed out that the character is not a rotten apple. It is his wife, Sonia, who seduces an impoverished lawyer, Kabir, and plots Rohit's murder for his money. He suggested my name for the role, saying that I would sizzle onscreen, that I was a dependable actor, and that my presence would confuse the audience and add to the intrigue. This time I didn't say 'no' even though I knew Bhatt saab would not be in the director's chair, having handed the baton over to Amit Saxena.

No sooner had I arrived in Pondicherry for the shoot than my regular make-up man, Suresh Dada, suffered a heart attack. He was like my elder brother, a workaholic, and responsible for all the looks I get credit for. I reached the set somewhat rattled and was informed that we would be shooting a lovemaking scene with Bipasha. While I didn't hesitate to make people's lives miserable onscreen, I was still shy of romance. In this case, my co-star was a relatively new actress which made the job doubly difficult. To make matters worse, Bhatt saab was not on the set because he was working on a song with the composer M.M. Kreem. I was out of my depth.

Fortunately, my dear friend Pooja, a sensitive film-maker herself, understood that for the film to work, Bipasha and I had to look comfortable with each other. Urging us to let go of our inhibitions, Pooja made us understand that while John Abraham's Kabir is overcome with lust for Sonia and can't stay away from her, what I feel for her is the possessive love of a husband who believes he means as much to her as she does to him. Thanks to Pooja, I pulled off a role that was out of my comfort zone. She made *Jism* easy for me, while Bhatt saab groomed me into the actor I am today. Thank you, sir.

10

I AM A BAD MAN

I owe the defining role of my life and career to Subhash Ghai.

One day, Subhash-ji met me and asked casually, 'What are you doing tomorrow?' With a string of hits—such as *Kalicharan*, *Vishwanath*, *Karz*, *Vidhaata*, *Hero*, *Meri Jung* and *Karma*—to his credit, which had earned him the tag of 'showman', his interest in me had my heartbeat accelerating with excitement. I told him I was shooting.

'What time do you have to be at the studio?' he asked.

'At ten in the morning, sir,' I replied, hoping I wasn't missing out on anything.

'Come home at 8 a.m. We will have breakfast together,' he instructed, before walking away.

Those days, if a film-maker invited you to breakfast, lunch, dinner, or even a drink it was understood that he had a role for you. In my hurry to grab it, I arrived at Subhash-ji's apartment on Bandra's Pali Hill, close to Mount Mary Church, half an hour early. He is a gracious host and his wife, Rehana bhabhi, offered me a variety of dishes, but food was the last thing on my mind. All I could think of was when Subhash-ji would broach the subject of the film. We chatted on many topics and as the time for my shoot neared, I began to panic. Finally, I got to my feet and told him I would have to leave for work.

He escorted me to the door, opened it and walked me to the elevator.

I couldn't believe that he was going to send me away without making me an offer. I waited, one eye on the elevator which was on its way up. 1 . . . 3 . . . 5 . . . 7 . . . 10 . . . 12 . . . 13 . . . 15 . . . 17 . . . Since he lived on the twentieth floor, we still had time, I reassured myself. He remained stubbornly silent and as the elevator drew closer, I finally burst out in desperation, 'Sir, what is my role? Or did you not call me for one?'

He smiled and replied, 'Your role is that you hate anyone who is good and every time you are onscreen, you announce your presence by saying, "I am a bad man."' I waited for him to elaborate, but he didn't. Meanwhile, the elevator arrived.

I got in, exclaiming incredulously, 'That's it, sir?'

He nodded, and with a twinkle in his eyes, quipped, 'Yes, that's it, Bad Man.'

The elevator whisked me away.

Subhash-ji is known to be cagey about his films, never giving out too much information to his actors or his protégés. He only revealed what was necessary for the actors to understand their characters. Being a writer himself, he always started out with the big picture in his mind and tweaked it as he went along. Sometimes he would write scenes on the morning of the shoot and on occasions, even rewrote them during the lunch break. This never hampered the filming. So, I did not get a script narration for *Ram Lakhan*, but learnt about 'Bad Man' Kesariya Vilayati through the little bits that Subhash-ji would let slip in during conversations. From this, I built up my own picture of the character and decided to give him a distinctive look.

I persuaded Madhav 'Tailor' to make me a Pathani suit topped by a waistcoat with gold buttons and a jacket. I carried what was to become my trademark blanket on my shoulder. Wigmaker Maliq designed a hairpiece for me that had spikes and a desi

mohawk. The beard and a moustache, which I could twirl at the
ends, was the handiwork of Suresh Dada. I then approached Nath
Gupta, whose photographs had landed me the role in *Avtaar*, to
do another photo session with me in this costume. He heard me
out and reasoned that he couldn't shoot a character like Kesariya
Vilayati on the road or in a park. 'We need an unusual location,'
he pointed out. So, we went scouting.

We eventually settled on action director Pappu Verma's
father's stables near Film City Studio. It housed several horses,
which Verma-ji hired out for film shoots, along with a collection
of weapons like daggers and axes. Nath Gupta took many
photographs of me there, which I showed Subhash-ji. He loved
the look and was wowed by my commitment. The backdrop we
had chosen also caught his eye and he asked me curiously, 'Where
did you take these pictures?' When I told him, he instructed his
brother, Ashok Ghai, who handled the production responsibilities,
to check out the location to see if it was available for a shoot.
I returned there again, this time with the legendary comedian
Mukri saab and Anil Kapoor. My experiment was such a hit that
from then onwards it became mandatory for Subhash-ji's banner,
Mukta Arts, to have a 'look' test for actors playing distinctive
characters.

My character had a long flashback with Kesariya Vilayati
killing Ram and Lakhan's father because he had refused to fall in
with the evil ploys of his cousins, played by Amrish Puri-ji and
Paresh Rawal. Raakhee-ji's character, Sharda, an eyewitness to her
husband's murder, vows revenge. The role had swag, panache and
larger-than-life drama, which Subhash-ji and the film's director
of photography, Ashok Mehta, magnified manifold onscreen.
Ashok-ji was a dear friend from my Marina Guest House days
and would cajole our director to let him shoot me from different
angles and try out new lighting techniques that would enhance
the menace 'Bad Man' exuded.

The revenge drama wrapped up towards the end of 1988 and was inching towards a Republic Day 1989 release. Those were the days of multi-theatre premieres and Subhash-ji had decided that all of us would assemble at his residence, leave our cars there, get into a mini bus he had hired for the evening, and go theatre-hopping. This way we would reach the cinemas at the same time without anyone getting caught in traffic and reporting late, or worse, not turning up at all. When Subhash-ji decides something, no one argues with him. So, we all clambered into the bus after him. Amrish Puri-ji, the heroines Dimple Kapadia and Madhuri Dixit, along with Anil and distributor Tolu Bajaj sat in front with Subhash-ji while I got a seat at the back. Jackie Shroff, who is a brooding introvert and always looking for a quiet corner, settled down beside me.

We went into the first theatre and to my surprise, we were greeted with cries of 'Bad Man'. This happened in the next three to four theatres as well and, suddenly, I was being invited to sit in front with Subhash-ji and our distributor. That's when I knew I had arrived.

The hysteria escalated with every passing day and when they were planning premieres in Delhi and Uttar Pradesh, distributors would call Subhash-ji directly and request him to bring me for sure. They were even okay taking only me along on promotional drives to small towns. 'Bad Man ko saath zaroor lana, he is very popular here,' became a constant refrain, which was music to my ears. The role made me a household name and I began to be known as 'Bad Man' for life. Thank you, Subhash Ghai.

Jackie is a good friend and after Ram Lakhan if any producer told him that they were contemplating casting me as the baddie, he would urge the film-maker, saying, 'Just take him, man, mazaa aa jayega, apun ka bahut banta hai.' I had met Jackie for the first time on the set of Raj N. Sippy's film, Andar Baahar, which had Anil and him in the lead. We had hit it off immediately. Two years after *Ram Lakhan*, I gunned him down, as he stood waist deep in the Ganga chanting mantras, in Subhash-ji's *Saudagar*.

That sequence was a lesson in direction, cinematography and editing. It was filmed in three different locations, at different times. I could not go on the outdoor shoot because I had another shoot commitment and Jackie, at the time, was not travelling out of Mumbai. So, Ashok-ji filmed Jackie's duplicate standing in the Ganga with shots of me loading the gun and pulling the trigger at Film City's helipad in Mumbai. Shots of Jackie standing waist-deep in another river when he is killed by my bullet were taken elsewhere. These shots were then stitched together on the editing table to make for a convincing sequence.

Saudagar, which bagged Subhash-ji the Filmfare Award for best director, was his most ambitious project, bringing together two legends, Dilip Kumar and Raaj Kumar. I played the villainous Baliram who is responsible for turning the childhood friends, Veer Singh aka Veeru and Rajeshwar Singh aka Raju, into bitter foes. Just as with *Ram Lakhan*, this role too went into a flashback. I did another photo shoot with Nath Gupta, detailing my two looks, young and old, and visually tracing the journey of my character, impressing Subhash-ji yet again. But since he had not asked me for my dates, I took off to Kenya to shoot Rajiv Rai's *Vishwatma*. There, I received an SOS call from Ashok Ghai-ji who had suddenly got dates from both Dilip saab and Raaj saab and wanted to start the film immediately with a scene featuring the two veteran actors and me. I was in trouble!

How was I going to fly back at such short notice from a foreign location? I was convinced *Saudagar* had slipped away from me. But Subhash-ji had a word with Rajiv Rai, who eventually let me off for a couple of days. I flew back to Mumbai and drove straight to Seth Studio where the unit was waiting to film the first scene. It was a dramatic point in the story when an enraged Raaj saab finally wisens up to my character's wicked ways and is determined

to finish Bali off. Dilip saab drags him away, pointing out that
by killing me he would only go to jail for life and that would be
foolish. This is the first time the relationship between the friends-
turned-foes thaws, and Subhash-ji was relying on the two legendary
actors and me to pull off the important scene. Excited to share the
frame with two actors I had idolized since childhood, I gave it all
I had. We wrapped up the scene in a few hours and I flew back to
Africa and *Vishwatma*.

Vishwatma is particularly close to my heart because it gave me
one of my memorable roles, with the quirkiest of names, Tapasvi
Gunjal, who dresses in the most garish purple, speaks in shuddh
Hindi and plays the flute! Equally important was my friend
Chunky Pandey's role in getting me to do the film. Chunky not
only persuaded me act in a film by one of my favourite directors
but also tricked me into shaving my moustache. In those years
I sported a moustache in all films because of continuity issues.
Getting to work with Rajiv Rai was however worth losing my
moustache for.

By the time I returned from Kenya, Manisha Koirala, the
beautiful Nepali girl whom Subhash-ji was introducing as Radha
and over whom the nation would go '*Ilu Ilu*' after *Saudagar*'s
release, had joined the action. Ashok Ghai-ji told me that Manisha
had returned to Mumbai for some work and requested me to bring
her to Mahabaleshwar in my car. I picked her up at Juhu and we
drove down to the shoot together. She is a sweet and friendly
girl, as fresh as a dew-sprinkled rose, pure and unaffected by the
manipulations of the industry. On the set, the two of us would
hang out with her young hero, Vivek Mushran, and Abhinav
Chaturvedi who had become a household name as Nanhe in the
television soap *Hum Log*. We spent most of our evenings together.
That was the beginning of my friendship with Manisha Koirala.

The film was like another acting school for me. There was
so much to learn from Dilip saab and Raaj saab. Just watching

them perform was a complete lesson. I had first met Dilip saab as Vinod Kumar, the upright, fearless newspaper editor in Yash Chopra-ji's drama *Mashaal*. Anil and I, along with Madan Jain and Babu Kumar, were the slum boys he tries to mentor, with Rajhans Singh, my acting school classmate, as our rival. We were a dedicated bunch of five, literally living on the chawl set at Rajkamal Studio, rehearsing our scenes for hours. Occasionally, we would visit real chawls to get a feel of the surroundings. Yash-ji was like an affluent, affectionate and artistic father who never lost his temper and also had a great sense of humour. He would sometimes invite us for a story or a music session at his place to expose us to other aspects of film-making. He was passionate about his craft and his zeal rubbed off on us.

I consider myself fortunate to have been part of two films directed by Yash-ji, *Mashaal* and *Vijay*. He was in many ways an institution and though my preference for villainous roles precluded my acting in his celebrated romantic films which seldom needed a villain to drive the narrative, I carry the learnings from these two films even today. No one portrayed romance onscreen as ethereally as Yash-ji and with his passing, love as we knew it in Hindi cinema, is forever lost.

We would go to Chor Bazaar, pick up second-hand clothes, and parade in them before him, hoping to get his approval. Javed Akhtar saab's scripts are very detailed and my character, Munna, was required to spit while speaking. Much as I tried, I couldn't do it and seeing my desperation, Rajhans even introduced me to a guy who sprayed you with a thin stream of saliva every time he spoke. It looked easy when I met him, but even though I chewed cloves and cardamom all day to whip up enough saliva, I couldn't emulate him. I only ended up with a burning sensation in my mouth and messed up my lines. Finally, I got Anil to set up an appointment for me with Javed saab, during which I confessed to him that I found it hard to spit between my lines as had been detailed in his script. Years later, I learnt that Javed saab found my confession cute, naïve and wonderfully sincere. That day, he looked at my troubled, young face, and said gently, 'Don't worry, do whatever comes to you naturally without bothering too much about what I have written.' I returned reassured that now no one would be asking for my head.

Yash-ji was an early riser and one day, we had already started shooting by the time Dilip saab arrived to film an important scene with us. We were in character—five angry, aggressive delinquents wondering why this man had not picked us out in an identity parade at the police station, gloating that he was perhaps afraid to take panga with us. It was a trolley shot, with us huddled in conversation and Dilip saab standing at the doorway of the restaurant listening to us before walking up to explain that one word from him would have put us behind bars and ruined our lives forever.

By then, all five of us knew every word, dot and comma in the script. When Dilip saab started rehearsing, I instantly noticed that some of the lines he was saying were not in the script. He had earlier told me that I had an interesting face, and affectionately putting an arm around my shoulder had enquired where I was from, obviously not recalling me as Sanjay Dutt's acting teacher from the dinner parties at Sunil Dutt saab's bungalow. That emboldened me to point out to him that he was saying his lines wrong. There was a sudden silence as Dilip saab sized me up. I was petrified.

'Beta, what am I saying wrong?' he asked quietly, and I parroted his lines which I knew by heart.

Smiling, he promised to say them correctly during 'take', then explained that while rehearsing, he simply absorbed the character and the setting while observing the other actors in the frame. 'The attention to lines comes later,' he informed. That was one of my first lessons in 'live' acting.

The scene continued, and Dilip saab who was uncomfortable talking down to Anil, suggested he stand up. This didn't go down well with the rest of us because we thought such a move would separate the two of them and cut us out of the frame. Anil, too, was hesitant until the till now amiable Dilip saab told him with steel in his voice, 'If you don't stand up on your own, I will grab you by your collar and haul you up.' He pointed out that such a gesture would not be amiss since his character doesn't want the boys to grow up into hardened criminals and will do everything to discipline them, even get physical if needed. With that, this living-walking institution set the tone of our relationship. Never again did we try to mess with him or teach him how to speak his lines.

The lessons weren't over yet. In another scene, my character, Munna, had to blind him with a handful of chilli powder, grab the briefcase of money he was carrying and run away, with him in hot pursuit. Eventually, he grabs hold of me and we grapple in the bushes near the railway tracks. While we were fighting, I discovered to my amazement that Dilip saab could lift me off the ground with the ease of a wrestler. He possessed brute strength.

We also quickly learnt that he played football like a pro. In one scene, where he challenges us to take the ball away from him, he left us dumbstruck as he deftly dribbled the ball and shot it cleanly into the net. Goal! The charming Dilip saab gave young actors like me not only a run for our money, but also free acting lessons.

I also picked up skills of a different kind by watching Subhash-ji interact with the two thespians during the *Saudagar* shoot. Dilip saab fondly called Subhash-ji 'Chief' while Raaj saab had given him the nickname 'General'. For the rest of us, he was the captain of the ship. When Subhash-ji had announced the film, many were openly sceptical about him ever completing it. It wasn't as if Dilip saab and Raaj saab were particularly difficult or temperamental, they just worked differently and they had made it clear to Subhash-ji that at this stage in their lives, they were not going to change themselves or their lifestyle for anyone.

Raaj saab, who was an early riser, would turn up for shoots between nine and ten in the morning. He would break at 1 p.m. for lunch and a siesta, returning to the set at 4 p.m. He was a stickler for time. He was always warm to me, but it was only after ten days of shooting that he recognized me as Gulshan Grover, the actor, and not one of the production hands.

Dilip saab started his day late. He would exercise, play a sport, have his brunch and then drive to the studio a little after noon. Subhash-ji barely had half an hour to forty-five minutes to get them together in a shot in the first session. There were times when Dilip saab, who enjoyed a chat, would alight from his car and stroll sedately towards the set, stopping en route for a powwow while we stood around shuffling our feet. Subhash-ji was patience personified, never hurrying him along. But I understood that since we were working on such a tight timeframe, I couldn't afford to mess up my shots. So, I made sure I was word-perfect, well-rehearsed and clued into every action and reaction.

Saudagar was a memorable journey, but what makes it unforgettable was a ride I took with Jackie one night. During that time, for two years, my friend had been told by his family astrologer that he should not spend even a night away from his home, no matter where he was shooting. So, Jackie would fly or drive back to Mumbai as soon as the sun went down, making the journey back to the set early the next day. He made sure he never inconvenienced his producers, always being the first guy on the set when we were filming in Mahabaleshwar. When we got to the set, we would find Jackie lying on a khatiya or sleeping in the car, but the moment he was called for a shot, he would jump up and be ready for action.

One evening, I also had to return to Mumbai for some urgent work and Jackie asked me to drive down with him. '*Chal bidhu, saath chalte hain*. We can chat on the way,' he urged. I was happy to hop in beside him as he took the wheel, dispatching his chauffeur to the back seat while I told mine to follow with my car. It was late at night, I was exhausted and half asleep after a long day at work. But within minutes, I was wide awake as Jackie pressed down on the accelerator and sped down the Ghats as if the Devil himself were behind us. I hung on for dear life as he took the turns on the near-empty road at breakneck speed, suddenly swinging off the highway into some narrow dirt road, reassuring me as we went bouncing down in the pitch dark that it was a short-cut that would get us home faster. Too terrified to protest, I simply nodded mutely, convinced that this was the last day of my life. Amazingly, his chauffeur slept through this ride, unconcerned.

Miraculously, I reached home in one piece and well before I had expected to. Jackie had cut down the six-hour drive to two and a half hours. He braked to a stop outside my apartment and with a cheerful smile told me that he would pick me up the next morning so that we could drive back together. I shook my head, hurriedly telling him I wouldn't be going that early since I had some work in town. I would see him at the shoot. He nodded, waved goodbye and zoomed off with a screech of tyres. I shuddered and staggered inside. Our ride, as brothers, continues to the day. Jackie will remain this Bad Man's amazing and inspiring buddy till the end of my life's journey.

11

REWIND, RECREATE, REINVENT

More than two decades after Subhash Ghai's 1980 musical blockbuster *Karz* opened in the theatres to the tune of '*Om Shanti Om*', Bhushan Kumar, the head honcho of the music label and production house T-Series, bought its remake rights. He signed Himesh Reshammiya to reprise the double role of Ravi Verma and Monty Oberoi, played by Rishi Kapoor-ji in the original. *Karzzzz* was the most talked-about film of 2008.

One day, as I was walking up the steps to my gym, I got a call from Bhushan offering me the role of the main villain, Sir Judah. I jumped at the chance to play this iconic character made memorable by the late Prem Nath-ji in the original. He rang off saying the film's director, Satish Kaushik, would set up a meeting with me.

Satish and I go back to my Delhi days when we would meet at intercollege fests. I would represent SRCC while he was from Kirori Mal College, both of us competing for the best actor award. From rivals we became good friends in Mumbai. During the narration, Satish told me that we would have to put our heads together and come up with something radically different that would wow the audience like Subhash-ji's voiceless villain who taps out his words on his whisky glass that are then translated by his nameless lackey, played by Mac Mohan-ji.

We started meeting frequently and watched the original *Karz* repeatedly to figure out what we could do with this stylish, gimmicky character without aping Prem Nath-ji. With a lot of help from Satish and a little bit of creative ingenuity of my own, I made my Sir Judah unique. I shaved my head, got myself a white goatee, and a metal arm with a musical synthesizer attached to it on which I would tap out my messages to my sidekick. Unfortunately, the film didn't work. But it marked the beginning of my friendship with the visionary Bhushan Kumar. I worked with his lovely wife Divya Khosla Kumar in her directorial debut *Yaariyan*. We shot the film in Guwahati and in freezing Darjeeling. My friendship with Bhushan and Divya remains strong and we will be collaborating on films together soon.

Despite my 'Bad Man' image and the occasional debacle, I remained one of the few 'baddies' who got the opportunity to go beyond this image because film-makers believed in my versatility and co-stars recommended me for interesting projects. One such film was Jagmohan Mundhra's *Bawandar*. The film was based on the true story of Bhanwari Devi, a low-caste Rajasthani woman who was raped for daring to inform the police about a child marriage happening in her community. I played the lawyer who goes against his own community to defend her in court.

Nandita Das, who played the protagonist Saanvri Devi (the names were changed for legal reasons), and I have a long history that goes back to Deepa Mehta's *Fire*. I was introduced to Nandita by the National Award-winning film-maker Prakash Jha. I, in turn, introduced Nandita to Deepa who was casting for the first film in her *Fire, Earth, Water* trilogy. I had already been confirmed to play Jatin, the younger brother who has an affair with a Chinese girl and shows little interest in his wife, Sita. Nandita, Tisca Chopra and Durga Jasraj were all well suited to play Sita, and I set up meetings with Deepa and all the three actresses at different times in my house. Deepa and Nandita hit it off instantly and since they both lived in Delhi, continued to meet. Then, suddenly, Nandita was in, and I was out. Apparently, they wanted a more conventional hero and I am told they had approached Kumar Gaurav before settling for Javed Jaffrey. I was bitterly disappointed and swore never to work with Deepa again.

Nandita and I met occasionally when she would fly down to Mumbai to shoot for Rakeysh Omprakash Mehra's psychological thriller *Aks*. Sometimes, I would also bump into her at Hotel Sun-n-Sand in Juhu where she was staying and where my gym was located.

Jagmohan-ji wanted me to play the bad lawyer in *Bawandar*, but having played similar roles in the past, I did not want to repeat myself. He then graciously handed me the script and asked me to pick a role of my choice. I immediately zeroed in on Ravi, the friend and interpreter of the foreign reporter, Amy, played by Laila Rouass. Five years after the rape of Saanvri Devi, Amy comes down to India to investigate this headline-grabbing case for her newspaper. Ravi helps Amy with her mission. Jagmohan-ji regretfully informed me that he had already committed this role to Rahul Khanna. I went through the script again and this time asked if I could play Saanvri Devi's lawyer, which Jagmohan-ji immediately agreed to.

My other good friend, Deepti Naval, enacted the role of Shobha Devi, a social worker with the government, who educates Saanvri Devi on social evils, urging her to raise her voice in protest against the age-old practice of child marriage prevalent in Rajasthan. The shoot in the desert was full of wonderful moments and *Bawandar* remains a special film for me. A critic, Ramachandran Srinivasan, praised me in his review, saying, 'Gulshan Grover's shattering and honest-to-earth performance makes you cry.'

While that is big praise, as any actor will tell you, the more difficult job is to make people laugh. During my visits to FTII in Pune, I would often meet the multitalented David Dhawan, who studied at the institute too but would often come down to Mumbai. He started his career as an editor, then moved to direction with his film *Taaqatwar*, which featured Govinda, Sanjay Dutt, Anita Raj and me. Five years later, we worked together on *Raja Babu*, which featured Govinda and Karisma Kapoor in the lead and boasted four actors who had made their name as screen 'villains'—Prem Chopra, Kader Khan, Shakti Kapoor and me— though Kader Khan and Shakti Kapoor were not playing baddies in this film. My dear friend David and his hero number one, Govinda, were making the box-office jingle and it felt good to be part of a success story.

Before *Raja Babu*, David and I worked on *Shola Aur Shabnam*, produced by the gutsy Pahlaj Nihalani. I enjoy a close rapport with Pahlaj-ji, starting with a shocking first meeting. Out of the blue one day, his line producer Chooga Mal landed up where I was shooting and said that Pahlaj-ji wanted me to do a guest appearance in his film and that too immediately. Though I was a struggling actor at the time, I was not so sure I wanted to do a cameo. Nevertheless, I went along with Chooga Mal to meet one of Bollywood's most successful producers with the intention of saying 'no'. But I ended up filming for a small role the same evening. This inability to say 'no' to him continues even today as he has always been very affectionate. I wanted to play the main villain in *Shola Aur Shabnam*, and Pahlaj-ji gave the role to me though he had paid an advance to Amrish Puri-ji. I worked in a number of films made by him, including *Aag Hi Aag*, *Gunahon ka Faisla*, *Aankhen* and many more.

Coming back to David Dhawan, I had discovered by then that while my Bud Spencer-lookalike director buddy was always smiling and would patiently hear our every suggestion, he would do only what he believed was right. As the notorious criminal, Kali Shankar, in *Shola Aur Shabnam* and baddie Banke in *Raja Babu*, I did exactly what David wanted me to do since the films were in his genre of expertise. They gave me some much-needed hits and proved my versatility as an actor. We went on to do other films like *Ek Aur Ek Gyarah*, *Mr & Mrs Khiladi*, *Eena Meena Deeka* and *Aankhen*. It was David Dhawan, someone I look up to as my brother, who taught me the importance of timing in acting, particularly in comic scenes.

Two years after *Raja Babu*, I was signed for *Raja Ki Aayegi Baraat*, which was also Rani Mukerji's debut film. Previously, I had worked in a few films produced by Salim Akhtar like *Doodh Ka Karz*, *Jigar* and *Police Officer*. One day, Salim bhai called me for a script narration. His wife served the most delicious meals and that along with the excitement of another challenging role, had me hurrying to his residence. He narrated the story of a young girl whose good deeds end with her getting raped. She moves the court, gets her rapist to marry her and eventually tames him with her love. Salim bhai wanted me to play Rani's father, Gyani Kartar Singh, who stands by her through her trials and trauma. I was really busy at the time, but I squeezed the film into my hectic schedule because while Salim bhai was a hard taskmaster, he was a wonderful person, finished his films on time, marketed them well, was a good paymaster and to top it all, this was a fantastic role.

On the sets of this film, I made Rani's acquaintance. She came from the famous Mukherjee family, but had no airs and worked hard like any other dedicated newcomer. I bonded with her mother Krishna-ji and her, and even today, Rani affectionately calls me Darji, short for Sardarji, after my character in the film. Once, at the Delhi airport, I walked into the executive office where celebrities used to be seated till the flight was announced, and found Priyanka Chopra, Rani and another actress there. As I stepped in, Rani's 'Darji' stopped me in my tracks. She ran towards me and gave me a hug. Her display of affection was heart-warming because Rani was a superstar by then.

She wanted me to play her father in Yash Chopra's comedy–thriller, *Bunty Aur Babli*, and sent the director, Shaad Ali, to me for a narration. It was a small role and while I was okay with playing Rani's father in *Raja Ki Aayegi Baraat*, a favourite with Sardars and Punjabis around the world even today, this role didn't have much meat. Shaad called Rani to tell her that I had reservations about the role. 'Darji, do it for me,' she entreated. I said 'yes' only because of her, but eventually I couldn't do it because of date problems. But Rani remains my favourite to this day. She did her first film with me, as did Manisha Koirala (*Saudagar*), Katrina Kaif (*Boom*), Bipasha Basu (*Jism*) and Kangana Ranaut (*Gangster*).

Another refreshingly different film which was strongly recommended to me was *I Am Kalam*. But I had no interest in a film produced by the Smile Foundation and directed by Nila Madhab Panda who had only made a few documentaries and short films till then. I only agreed to a twenty-minute meeting because I didn't want to refuse the film-makers outright. I had even instructed my staff to come into the living room after twenty minutes to tell me that a few guests had arrived and were waiting in the next room. Halfway through the narration, despite my obvious reluctance to do the film, I was in tears. The story was engaging and entertaining despite touching on dark subjects like child labour and education. Also, the intention of the film-makers was so pure that I just couldn't bring myself to say 'no' directly.

The story is about a young boy who is so inspired by A.P.J. Abdul Kalam that he not only changes his name to Kalam, but also follows our late President's life's course. His tenacity reminded me of my modest childhood and the boy I had once been.

I called my son Sanjay in LA and narrated the story to him. 'Dad, do it,' he urged. The problem, I knew, was that if I was going to charge them my usual fee, it would eat into their entire budget. So, I told the film-makers that I would think about the offer. They left me some material to read. Three hours later, after discussing with Sanjay, I called them, shocking them with my decision to do the film for free. I did not even take along my make-up man and other staff. My only request was that they wrap up my portions in one schedule because I had no dates to spare.

When I reached Bikaner airport, I got into the car they had sent, and was driven to a five-star hotel where I had stayed earlier. I asked the assistant about the rest of the team's whereabouts and was informed that they were staying at a modest hotel. I told him to take me there. My decision bridged the distance between 'me' and 'them'. It also saved the film-makers plenty of money. The young assistants would be up all night, drinking, singing and dancing, so I didn't get much sleep but that didn't bother me. Also, since we shot some scenes in the hotel itself, a table or a chair would suddenly become a prop and be carried out of my room.

I played the owner of the dhaba where Chhotu works. There was no trailer or vanity van with air-conditioned comfort as the make-up team from Delhi worked on me. I crammed myself in with twenty others into a small box-room where Chhotu and the other boy slept in the film. It had a loud and rusty fan, which would be switched off during a shot as we were working with sync sound and the softest noise could mess up a take. What was worse was there was no bathroom nearby. So, to relieve myself, I had to take a long walk into the desert, away from fans who were constantly taking pictures on their cell phones. The film unit was expecting me to crack. However, the talent around me and the film itself, as also Nila Madhab's dedication, rendered these inconveniences trivial.

I was rewarded for my patience and perseverance when I bagged the best actor awards at both the Los Angeles and Houston Film Festivals, and also the Stardust Awards in India. I was later told that I had also been a strong contender for the National Award. J.P. Dutta, who had made *Border* and *LoC*, and who was head of the jury that year, told me that I had narrowly missed out on the coveted national honour.

Soon after the film's release, Pratibha and her father Lal Krishna Advani, the doyen of Indian politics who served as deputy prime minister under Atal Bihari Vajpayee, organized a special screening of *I Am Kalam* in the capital. There were around 500 guests present and Dada Advani-ji introduced me as his daughter's friend, raving about this 'inspiring' film and my performance. Pratibha and I met a decade ago during the course of an interview for her talk show and thanks to her, I had many opportunities of spending time with Dada Advani-ji. What a learning experience that has been. He keeps inspiring me in every way.

I Am Kalam was a very special film. Wherever I travelled with the film, be it to Germany, Italy, America or Spain, I would find mothers in tears for little Chhotu and his tribulations. It is reactions like these that make my job as an actor emotionally satisfying and creatively satiating. Nila Madhab Panda is a very talented director and I am so glad I worked in his film, albeit because of my son insisting that I do it. I have to admit that Sanjay has more cinematic sense than I do.

12

A PASSAGE TO HOLLYWOOD

For many years I have been a part of Bollywood concert tours across the globe which pack in crowds of non-resident Indians (NRIs), along with plenty of locals, and whip up unbelievable euphoria. These tours included shows with lots of songs and dances, stretching for over a month and a half. They were usually held in the United Kingdom, the United States and Canada, enabling the Indian diaspora to see their favourite stars up close and personal. I wanted to experience those screams of delight for myself and the opportunity arose because of my friend, international event organizer and promoter Farhath Hussain. The journey started with a tour with Jeetendra, Sanjay Dutt, Sridevi and Neelam. The next concert was with Shah Rukh Khan, Mithun Chakraborty, Sunny Deol, Karisma Kapoor and Meenakshi Seshadri. This was followed by tours with the two Khans—Shah Rukh and Aamir— along with Sonali Bendre, Urmila Matondkar and Mamta Kulkarni. Once, I was also in a team that included Shah Rukh, Akshay Kumar, Juhi Chawla and Kajol. I also travelled with other stars like Suniel Shetty, Raveena Tandon and Mahima Chaudhry.

It feels good to know that I was the first of the baddies to get an opportunity to perform at these shows. I went on these cross-continental runs every year, going out of my way to be a part of them because they gave me the opportunity to travel with the family. There was also plenty of adulation and a strange kind of thrill that came from the electrifying energy of fans who were watching you perform live and whose feedback was instant and vociferous.

Shah Rukh Khan was the biggest draw and got the loudest cheers. The other stars were fantastic too and my act, with synchronized sound effects and applause-worthy dialogues penned by Mahesh Bhatt saab, was also a huge hit. Shah Rukh's wife Gauri and her friends, along with the wives of the Morani brothers, Ali, Karim and Mohammed, who organized these shows with Farhath Hussain, would sit backstage for most of the show because they had already seen it all before. But as soon as my name was announced, they were out in the front, just as excited as the rest. My act was positioned prominently in the order of performances and I got a lot of support from not just the spectators but also my fellow performers, particularly from Shah Rukh. He would urge the organizers to rope me in, saying, 'Gulshan Grover has a huge fan following outside India and his act is fantastic!' He was also the reason I got to be a part of these tours every year.

I give all credit for my unique act to my friend, the late actor–director Mazhar Khan, who designed it, and to Lollypop, and later Ganesh Hegde, who choreographed it. While we were studying at Roshan Taneja's acting school, Mazhar had excelled in the 'movement' class and his talent came in handy when he started doing shows with another classmate, Vicky (Wasim Khan). I played a supporting role in some of their shows, although my focus was always on drama rather than dance given my two left feet. When I got an opportunity to travel abroad for these Bollywood concerts, I requested Mazhar to pick out some interesting music for me. He heard the popular Hindi film tracks I had brought along and told me to throw them away and book a recording studio instead for four hours. 'I will give you something original and distinctive,' he promised.

The four hours stretched to four days. Mazhar was at his creative best and there were days when he would discuss a piece of music for an entire session while I sat there nervously biting my nails and counting the money I had to pay the studio. Shashi Ranjan would often drop by and lightly reprimand him, 'You will be at this for ten more days.' At times, he would ask me to run down to Mahesh Bhatt saab and get him to write a monologue for a baddie which he was happy to. Mazhar compensated me for my time with a mind-blowing act, complete with me digging out a cigarette lighter in the middle, the sizzling sound effects of the flame flaring up amplified on stage by the speakers, and footsteps, screams, gunshots and the clanging of chains when I am tied down, interspersed with my dialogues. It also had me, a menacing villain, suddenly breaking into a dance to the most romantic songs, attempting the signature moves of the Khans, Salman and Shah Rukh, Akshay and Amitabh Bachchan-ji, which never failed to get the audience rolling in the aisles.

The shows kept getting bigger and better every year, with new additions and improvisations. Till Mazhar's untimely death in 1998, he orchestrated my big production, with my chauffeur making frequent trips back home during the recording to pick up more money. I didn't grudge the expense because the feedback was always overwhelming. My face was plastered on every publicity poster and in every city we visited, there would be crowds of fans screaming my name and queueing up for autographs. I came to realize that in the West, they don't differentiate between a hero and a villain unlike India where the wife of an industrialist-friend down south was admonished by her friends for going out to dinner with me a couple of times. 'Couldn't you have found anyone better than that badmash?' they told her, pointing out that Vinod Khanna or even Sanjay Dutt would have been a more appropriate companion. I understood that their dislike wasn't for the person I was, but the image I projected onscreen. Still, it was encouraging when young fans abroad showered as much love on the 'Bad Man' as they did on the 'Good Guy' because public perception in the West is shaped by your performance and little else.

I was encouraged by the applause, but more than that these tours gave me the opportunity to experience the West. During that month and a half run, all of us watched close to thirty films in the theatres. I remember going to the movies with Shah Rukh, Juhi, Aamir, Akshay, Mahima and so many others. Watching films with an American audience gave me an insight into what audiences in the West liked and wanted to watch.

For a long time, I had been thinking of taking my craft to the next level and expanding my range as an actor. The shows gave me a better understanding of a global audience and I felt the desire to experiment. It's in my DNA to push the envelope, make the impossible possible. I had started my education at a small government school but had graduated from one of the country's most prestigious colleges. With a master's degree in economics and the world of commerce beckoning me, I had strayed towards fine arts. Then, even though I did not fit into the image of the conventional Bollywood baddie and the odds were hugely stacked against me, I had persevered and carved a niche of my own in the Hindi film industry. Offers were pouring in, along with admiration from Indian fans, but that wasn't enough. It's logical for any talent to crave international recognition after having attained a certain stature at the national level, and I was no different. I wanted to spread my wings beyond Bollywood, which had given me so much, into Hollywood.

But it wasn't easy. The Indian contacts who brokered introductions between actors here and their Western counterparts, as also those who interacted with the foreign studios frequently, had given the latter to believe that only actors from parallel cinema and theatre were genuinely talented and worthy of international exposure. Bollywood stars were unprofessional prima donnas and mediocre artistes given to throwing starry tantrums. We were like the naked children in an impoverished family who had to be quickly tucked away out of sight when guests came calling. This had put off the casting agents in the West and so we got no more than five minutes with them when they visited India. But actors who worked in 'art' films back then enjoyed long breakfast and dinner meetings with them. This rankled because I knew that this perception was far from the truth. So, I set out on a one-man mission to prove that our mass popularity didn't make us lesser actors.

Before me, path-breakers like Sabu, popularly known as the 'Elephant Boy'; Kabir Bedi, whose hit Italian television series, *Sandokan*, had taken him to American shores; Saeed Jaffrey, who was the favourite of Oscar-winning British film-maker duo Ismail Merchant and James Ivory; and Persis Khambatta, who went glamorously bald for a role in *Star Trek: The Motion Picture*, had taken the creative leap and made a name for themselves in Hollywood and international cinema. But they had to relocate to the US to work there and had ceased to be Indian actors. I was the first mainstream actor from India to make the transition from Bollywood to Hollywood without relocating or leaving the Hindi film industry and Indian cinema. It was national pride that kept me rooted to my land, while a burning desire to give Hindi commercial cinema its due took me away from it. So far, the West had only seen the films of our great masters like Satyajit Ray and Mrinal Sen. I wanted them to appreciate the talent of Amitabh Bachchan, Shah Rukh Khan, and yes, 'Bad Man' Gulshan Grover too.

During one of my concert tours with Shah Rukh, Juhi, Akshay and Kajol one of the stops was Los Angeles (LA) where we had a show at the Shrine Auditorium, a prestigious event venue. Wherever we went, we performed over the weekend. We got Monday to Thursday off to do our own thing and usually left for the next city on Wednesday. This meant that I had two days in LA to understand Hollywood better, a really short time for such a tall order. But as luck would have it, a few NRI friends I was dining with informed me that the producers of *The Second Jungle Book: Mowgli & Baloo* were scouting for an Indian actor and asked me if I would like them to fix an appointment with the director Duncan McLachlan. I jumped at the opportunity. A meeting was set up at Century City in Beverley Hills where coincidentally, my son, Sanjay, who worked as studio producer and studio executive at MGM for almost fifteen years, would also have his office in later years.

Back then, I was a tourist in LA and clueless about Century City. I called Tabrez Noorani, the line producer of Danny Boyle's Oscar-winning drama *Slumdog Millionaire* and the director of *Love Sonia*. Tabrez had been an assistant to Mazhar during his directorial *Gang* and was like a younger brother to me. When I asked him for directions, he offered to drop me. He left only after I had assured him that I would be able to find my way back to the hotel.

As usual, I was early and went to the washroom to freshen up. There, I noticed a Caucasian gentleman staring at me. His scrutiny made me uncomfortable and even as I was wondering who he was, he surprised me by suddenly blurting out, 'Are you Gulshan Grover?'

I nodded and asked him how he knew me. With a laugh he said that he was Duncan McLachlan whom I had come to meet.

'How did you recognize me?' I asked, surprised, and Duncan told me that my friends who set up the meeting had asked him to look out for an exotic Indian gentleman with hypnotic eyes. He ushered me to his office, his eyes still glued on me, and after about an hour of intense conversation, offered me the role of Buldeo, the main villain in the film. As the title suggests, this was not the 2003 animated film, *The Jungle Book 2*, but a live action adaptation of Rudyard Kipling's *The Jungle Book* for the screen by Bayard Johnson and Matthew Horton.

I was astounded to land the role of the main villain. Duncan admitted that he loved my hypnotic, shifty eyes. How could I tell him that they seemed shifty because I was unsure of the reception and had been unable to look him in the eye. He gave me a copy of the script to read, took my contact number, asked me where I was headed and offered to drop me back to my hotel. I returned to my suite and walked straight towards the side table which served as a makeshift temple. As instructed by my mother, I always travel with pictures of gods and I offered a prayer of thanks. After that, I finally smiled to myself, thinking, 'Crashing into Hollywood is this easy!'

The makers confirmed the offer after a couple of days. I was exultant. The story, set in 1890 India, revolved around Mowgli, a ten-year-old orphan brought up in the jungle by his animal friends. While fleeing from Sher Khan, the tiger who had killed his father, he catches the eye of Harrison, a circus scout, who wants to take him to America and put him to work. Buldeo is a wealthy jungle guide and Mowgli's paternal uncle who secretly wants to kill the boy and grab his inheritance. He leads Harrison and Chuchundra into the jungle after Mowgli. I discovered to my delight that I had sixty-seven important scenes and a fight in the climax.

I asked Duncan and the producers to let me know when I was expected to start shooting because I needed to plan my schedule back home accordingly given that I was working on multiple projects. I returned to India, excited and triumphant. Initially, there was an exchange of encouraging faxes between us, but soon after there was complete radio silence. I was at the time shooting for *Yes Boss* and discussed this with my co-star and friend Aditya Pancholi who advised me to head for LA to meet the producers.

He was also gracious enough to lend me money for my ticket. After wrapping up my shoot in Switzerland, I flew to LA and dropped by their office to enquire what was amiss. The filmmakers wouldn't meet me and I came back home, disappointed and disheartened. Eventually a fax arrived, informing me that the film's distributor, Columbia TriStar Pictures, did not want to take on an actor unknown to Hollywood for such a significant part and had decided to replace me with an American star. They apologized for the unfortunate turn of events and hoped to work with me in future. A dream that had materialized so quickly now lay shattered.

Heartbroken, I went about my Bollywood assignments stoically. Till suddenly, I was surprised by a call from the co-producer, Peter Shepherd, telling me that they wanted me back in the film. Hope soared. Without beating around the bush, I told Peter that I would be happy to be a part of the team. The surprises weren't over yet. 'Great, we want you to join the shoot tomorrow,' he stated, and dashed my hopes once again. I told him that this would be difficult because I had several films on the floor. He explained that they were also in a bit of a fix because they had started shooting with the American star despite the director being unhappy with their choice. They had even forced them to shoot one more day after which Duncan had threatened to walk out, saying he only wanted the actor with the hypnotic, shifty eyes. So, finally, they had decided to surrender to the director's vision. 'Please bail us out,' Peter requested. Still bemused by the offer, I asked that this time they put it down in writing and told Peter I would get back to him the next morning. Within minutes I got a fax confirming the offer. Peter also instructed me not to cut my hair, which was long at the time, so it would match that of Mowgli's in the film since I played his uncle.

I was in a quandary now as I had committed to an outdoor shoot of Aziz Mirza bhai's *Yes Boss* and had no idea how to wriggle out of the assignment at the last minute. Besides *Yes Boss*, there were a few other shoots in progress as well, including a film directed by Harry Baweja. There was only one man who could help me out.

That night, I sought out Shah Rukh, the leading man of *Yes Boss*, and showed him the fax I had received from the Hollywood film-makers, admitting that there was no way I could explain the situation to Aziz bhai or the film's producer, Ratan Jain, who would be left in the lurch if I suddenly opted out. 'What should I do?' I asked him.

'My friend, you go, I'll take care of everything here, no one will question your decision,' Shah Rukh assured me.

I couldn't believe my ears. I had come to the studio desperate for help, but to actually get it from the Badshah of Bollywood was really something. Still unsure, I asked, 'Should I send the Hollywood producers a fax tomorrow morning regarding my commitment?'

Shah Rukh was magnanimous.

'Go ahead, become a star in Hollywood,' he urged.

When Shah Rukh commits to something, he always delivers, and this time too he did not disappoint. I don't know how he did it, whether he made good the losses to the Jains or somehow convinced Aziz bhai to keep my scenes for later, but one thing I know for sure, I owe the start of my Hollywood journey to the Badshah of Bollywood. Without his intervention I would never have been able to give the nod to *The Second Jungle Book: Mowgli & Baloo* and might have lost out on a second chance of wooing the West. I flew out the next morning to join the Hollywood unit which was filming in Kandy Mountain in Sri Lanka.

Here, I would like to hit the rewind button and take you back to the time after the release of *Baazigar*. I had said in a television interview that I believed it was unwise of Shah Rukh to experiment with the role of an anti-hero so early in his career, attributing the gamble to a desire for quick gains and instant fame. The next day, when I was shooting at Filmistan Studio and sitting outside with Veeru Devgan-ji and a few others, Shah Rukh walked up to me and said with a confidence rarely found in a newcomer, 'I did not do this film for quick gains and instant fame but because I want to take the hero's role forward. I am not a fly-by-night operator; I am in this industry for life.' His supreme self-assurance left me speechless. Veeru-ji and the rest of the team observed our interaction apprehensively, believing that King Khan and Bad Man would fight and maybe there would be an exchange of fisticuffs. But it only cemented a lifelong bond and eventually led to my superstar friend helping me live out my Hollywood dream.

In Sri Lanka, the first four days were restricted to look tests, script readings and discussions with the team. Everyone was cordial, but I sensed a simmering hostility among the Hollywood crew. They were wondering about this actor unknown to them who was filling in the shoes of a big Hollywood star. I could feel the cold vibes as I went through my costume fittings and watched my hair being set. Finally, it was time to face the camera. We were shooting at a railway station that day and, to the unit's amazement, I turned out to be a familiar face in the island country as was evident from the number of fans hanging around the set, queuing up for my autograph and photograph. They were surprised by all the attention I was receiving. But every member had a copy of the script and had read it several times. They had an idea of the kind of actor required to play this significant part and despite my popularity in Sri Lanka, many were unconvinced that I was the one.

In the past, I have had people doubting my ability to pull off iconic parts and I had surprised them by stealing the thunder and winning awards. With the confidence that comes from knowing that you are good at your job, I strolled towards the camera. The first shot was being set, and I noticed that everyone was rushing to the monitor to see for themselves why the director thought I was special. I faced the camera and as Duncan shouted 'Action', I started to perform. As the day progressed, I could see the shine of approval in the eyes of the rest of the unit too and as the clouds of doubt cleared, sunny smiles broke through. By the end of the first day, everyone had warmed up to me. I knew then that I was on a good wicket. Phew!

Hollywood is a melting pot of talent and it draws actors from across the world. Over the decades, I have learnt that the only way to earn the respect of your co-workers in the West is to do your job and do it well. It doesn't matter how many people recognize you on the street or how impressive your resume is. You could be a big star in your country but in the eyes of Hollywood you are only as good as your performance in front of the camera. Fumble with your lines, forget your cues, turn up late on the set or not show up at all for the shoot and you are persona non grata.

Going by the reactions of everyone, I had passed the acid test with flying colours, but I was still a virtual prisoner in Sri Lanka. On the day I landed, while introducing me to the staff and showing me my room, Peter suddenly asked me for my passport. When I asked him why he wanted it, he told me frankly that they had heard horror stories about Bollywood actors who, lost and vulnerable in an alien country, would run back home without notice. I realized that the work ethics of our actors were suspect and had made them question our reliability. As a representative of my country and the film fraternity, I had to prove not just my talent as an actor, but also convince them that our sincerity and professionalism were beyond doubt.

Peter had told me the call sheet would have all the information, including the number of the car sent to take me to the location, the name of the driver and the time of pick-up. This service was extended to every member of the unit who was put up at the five-star hotel in Kandy. But since it was a heritage hotel, the driveway wasn't too large. To avoid an early-morning jam that would inconvenience the other guests, the chauffeurs were instructed to wait no longer than thirty seconds for a pick-up. Usually, there were not more than three people in a car, but even if only two arrived on time, the chauffeur was instructed to leave for the location. The person left behind could drive down with the production bosses.

Peter was in the lobby every morning with a cup of coffee in his hand. I learnt later that he was there specifically to keep an eye on me and ensure that I showed up and left on time. Having heard stories about our notorious Indian Standard Time (IST), he had expected me to be late and keep everyone waiting. He was relieved that every day I was in the lobby before time.

My punctuality and on-camera performance quickly endeared me to Peter and the rest of the team, but it didn't get me back my passport. After a few days, faxes from my Indian producers started arriving at the office in the hotel, entreating me to return home quickly so they could complete their films. I requested Peter to let me make a quick dash back so I could complete my commitments. But he turned me down, explaining that *The Second Jungle Book: Mowgli & Baloo* was a big-budget studio production and fully insured so they didn't want to take a chance. 'What if your car meets with an accident? Our outdoor would be hit for a six and we would be left bleeding. I'm sorry but I cannot even allow you to return for the premiere of a film,' he rued. They wouldn't even let me do a stunt that required me to fall, arguing that if I hurt myself, filming would grind to a halt. And so, I stayed on in the Lankan rainforest with Mowgli till it was time to wrap up.

13

AN ACTOR IN TRANSIT

Hollywood, which in those days was not even on the horizon of Bollywood actors, was finally within reach. It seemed like an impossible dream come true. On many mornings, I would wake up wondering if it were really happening or if I were still asleep. But the first print of *The Second Jungle Book: Mowgli & Baloo* was ready and after the maiden screening, everyone who was there, including the sceptical distributors, Columbia TriStar Pictures, who had once been more keen on an American actor, agreed that I had nailed it as Buldeo and was one of the film's highlights. It was a proud moment for me. In my mission to explore new worlds, to boldly go where no mainstream Indian actor had gone before, I had made the first breakthrough. The film released in the US on 16 May 1997, and I was invited to LA for the theatrical release. I went to the theatres with my director Duncan McLachlan and it was a real thrill signing autographs for kids who were not Indians. That was a first for Bollywood's 'Bad Man'.

Later in the year, I received another invitation, this time to Las Vegas, for the DVD release. Back then, DVDs were big business and various studios would come to Las Vegas for the annual convention to release their home videos. Besides the fans, there were many video library owners from around the world present at the gala who, if impressed, would place bulk orders. Posters were put up and memorabilia distributed, there were live performances and meet-and-greet sessions with the stars. Jamie Williams, who played Little Mowgli, and I were the crowd-pullers for our film. Our presence at the annual fair had been widely publicized in the local newspapers. There were also life-size hoardings all around the venue and fans queued up in hundreds for our autographs. Specially shot photographs of us had been taken earlier. Carrying the title of the film and the studio's logo, these photographs were widely distributed at the venue. Jamie and I were seated on the dais and given marker pens. Fans who bought DVDs of our film lined up with these photographs for us to sign. So, instead of getting our autographs on scraps of notepaper, discarded tissues and used napkins, fans received a one-of-its-kind film memorabilia. Being a commerce student, I appreciated such marketing gimmicks and returned from my trips abroad ready to sell these ideas to film-makers back home during movie promotions.

I was in Las Vegas for two days and made two appearances a day. That year, the American–Mexican actress Salma Hayek, widely acclaimed for films like *Desperado* and *From Dusk till Dawn*, had featured in the American romcom *Fools Rush In*, also distributed by Columbia Pictures, and they had invited her to Las Vegas to promote her film as well. Salma was scheduled for an appearance immediately after Jamie and me. Having come a few minutes early, she was impressed with the response we generated despite being new faces in the US. When the president of publicity, Fritz Friedman, introduced us, telling her I was a popular Bollywood actor, she evinced keen interest in India. I will always remember her as an elegant stunner whose beauty was not marred by even the slightest hint of arrogance.

Later, Salma was to play my wife in *The Driver*, a Hollywood film directed by William Henry Duke Jr. aka Bill. The American actor, director, writer and producer had directed films like Whoopi Goldberg's *Sister Act 2: Back in the Habit*, *Hoodlum* and had been nominated for a Palme d'Or for *A Rage in Harlem*. He had also starred with Arnold Schwarzenegger in *Commando* and *Predator* and helmed popular television series like *Cagney & Lacey* and *Hill Street Blues*. Unfortunately, the project fell through, but Salma remains one of my favourite stars.

All the adulation I received after *The Second Jungle Book: Mowgli & Baloo* made me believe that I had arrived in Hollywood too, but the bubble quickly burst. I have often noticed that when any of our home-grown stars fly off to the West, their Bollywood careers take a hit. So, did mine.

Film-makers back home weren't sure they could trust me any more despite my professionalism. They were afraid that I would dump them the minute I landed a Hollywood film. Many of them jumped to the conclusion that I had moved to LA for good, and without even checking with my manager, didn't bother approaching me. A few stayed away, apprehensive that I would demand too much money now that I was earning in dollars. Others were worried that I would suddenly find our studios dirty and lacking in amenities after my stint aboard, like many NRIs, and make their lives hell. And there were still others who feared that I would ask them too many questions about my role and the film, to which they would have no answers because back then many of them worked without bound scripts, with scenes being written the previous night or even on the day of the shoot on the set. When my photographs with Goldie Hawn and Bruce Willis started appearing in the press, it only added to their misgivings.

There were many colleagues who were genuinely happy for me, but I also began to hear snide remarks, made within my earshot, at the studios. Some of my colleagues even ridiculed me openly, wondering why I would be foolish enough to leave behind a lucrative career in India to start from scratch in another film industry across the seven seas. Since many of these carping Cassandras had no idea that I had dabbled in theatre during my college days in Delhi or that I was a trained actor who had worked as a teacher in an acting school for almost a decade, my reasons for the big 'switch' were subject to much speculation. Many assumed that it was the lucre that had lured me away.

I had been taught in college to aggressively market a brand and I did everything possible to enhance my 'Bad Man' image, not just onscreen but also at public events. But in the privacy of my home and with those close to me, I remained the same staid Gulshan. My popularity as a Bollywood baddie did not stop my yearning to evolve as an actor and venture into new avenues. That's what took me to the West. But my confidence quickly faded as the offers back home started to dry up. There were times when I would fly in from LA but say that I had been in Hyderabad because, unsure of the reactions, I was afraid if I told my colleagues the truth, it would only put them off. It was strange, when I should have been celebrating my leap forward with my fraternity, I was trying to pretend it hadn't happened.

In Hollywood, you can't make any inroads without an agent or a manager and those I connected with were unwilling to represent me because I was an actor who was always in transit. They wanted me to leave my country and settle down in LA, as others had done before me, so I would always be available for meetings and auditions, which, they pointed out, could happen at an hour's notice and slip out of my fingers in the time it took me to fly down from India. 'Apply for a green card, get yourself a permanent address here, that's the first step,' I was advised.

Others even suggested that I take a weekly crash course, or one that was a few months in duration, at one of the many acting schools in LA to learn how to make an impression at auditions. At these classes, some guy who had done a handful of films would take US$200 to guide you on how to pass the Hollywood acid test. 'Wear clothes like these . . . Look the person in the eye . . . Fold the pages properly . . .' The instructions, often banal and not offering anything I hadn't known, would go on and on. After all these tips, they would read the scene with me and tell me how to act it out. Back in my country, I was a big star, but in the US, I was being asked to learn acting like a novice. It was ironic!

I was also directed to acting cafés where if I hung out, I was told, I stood a good chance of catching the eye of a casting agent. It reminded me of my struggling days in Mumbai and all the posturing outside Pamposh Restaurant and in the Mehboob Studio car park. The ploy hadn't worked in Bollywood and I knew it wouldn't work in Hollywood either.

I had no desire to go down that road even if other actors of Indian origin before me had taken this advice and it had worked for some of them like Saeed Jaffrey, that brilliantly versatile British–Indian actor who migrated to the US, and one of my favourites, Kabir Bedi, who relocated after wooing Italy as the pirate Sandokan in the television mini-series in the mid-1970s. I met Kabir and his then wife Nikki many times in LA. He was always very encouraging and generous with his advice. He even gave an interview saying that he respected me for taking this bold step and trying to make inroads into Hollywood despite being a big star back home, courage my colleagues back home lacked, not wanting to leave their secure stardom and comfort zone.

In the early days, like so many of my Bollywood counterparts, some of them A-listers here, I did go for a few auditions. But I found them to be lacking in creativity and humiliating. Forty or fifty actors would gather at a Hollywood studio, casting building, or a casting agent's office. After you registered yourself, you were handed some sheets detailing the scene you were to act out. On occasions, your agent would have faxed you the scene before the audition so you were better prepared. You were then directed to a room upstairs where other hopefuls were waiting. And in that instant, you became a face in the crowd.

Standing or sitting in a corner, you learnt your lines, praying you wouldn't fumble. You worked on your moves even as you watched the other actors, many far from perfect for the part, do the same. Everyone was vying for the same role and the cold vibes were all too evident. Exuding presence and confidence that came from the hundreds of films in my kitty, I posed a serious threat to them. I could almost hear them thinking, 'God, if you are in my corner, let that bloke suffer a heart attack this very moment and die before his name is called so he doesn't cut me out of a lifetime's chance.'

The competitiveness, so blatantly palpable, made me blanch, and on many occasions, I'd make a dash for the washroom. When I asked one of the aides where it was located, I would be pointed to one on the ground floor that had a handwritten notice and lots of instructions, both outside and inside the loo, including 'Don't carve scenes in my toilet.'

If I wanted to wet my parched throat, I would be pointed to another notice. I could get water, but the coffee was only for the staff. And so, the humiliation piled up till my name was finally called. I would step into a room, smile stiffly and get down to the job of acting out the scene with a junior casting agent filming me, rather indifferently, often with the light all wrong. No one in the room was interested in conversation and wanted me to start on my lines immediately. At times, all I heard from them was 'That's good' or 'Thanks' or 'Bye' before I left the room. This tape, often heavy with static because no one had thought to muffle the background noises, would be seen by others higher up in the order, between sips of coffee and a lot of chatter. No matter how sincere your screen test was, these guys had little interest in a stranger. I would like to believe a lot of this has changed for the better now.

The process was all the more demeaning for someone like me who was a superstar back home. On one occasion, I turned up for an audition to find myself in the midst of 'fans'. They were mostly NRIs living in LA. Some had come down from Orlando, Arizona and New York to try their luck. All of them had regular jobs and had come to audition for a lark. When I strode into the room and took a chair, they recognized me immediately. From the puzzled looks on their faces, I knew they were wondering what a star like Gulshan Grover was doing there as they queued up for my autograph. To begin with, they believed I had swung by to meet the boss, but when they realized that I too was in the running for the same role of an 'Indian guy', I could clearly see that they were disillusioned. Unable to face them, I had turned tail and ran out of the studio. This meant a long wait at the corner before my ride arrived.

After that, I told my agents that while I was ready for the grind and game for a 'look' test, I refused to be auditioned with forty others. I promised that I would fly down if a role was worth the time and effort. Today, our actors like Priyanka Chopra are successfully dividing their time between Hollywood and Bollywood, but back then, it was unheard of for Indian actors to fly halfway across the world for a film every few months. I reiterated that I would not leave my country and quit mainstream Hindi cinema and relocate to the US to focus exclusively on Hollywood. I pointed out that the super-hit romcom *Notting Hill*'s Brit export, Hugh Grant, still lived in London. I argued that Nicole Kidman from Down Under made frequent trips out of Australia. I reminded them that Jean Reno, a French actor of Spanish descent, lived in Paris and made French, Italian, Spanish, Japanese and English films.

I was told that these actors had featured in big-ticket movies and being familiar faces at prestigious film festivals, were known to studio bosses while my cinema and I had yet to make an impression in Hollywood's corridors of power. It was sad. I had done thousands of hours of work, but since no one in LA had watched a Hindi film on VHS or DVD, and we were still in the pre-Internet era, my popularity and performances were lost to them, as was the talent our cinema boasted.

Later, when my son started working at MGM Studio, he made me proud by organizing private screenings for Hollywood bigwigs to acquaint them with our cinema. I also carried films with me during my frequent trips to LA. My suitcase had more DVDs of Indian films than clothes. This resulted in me being stopped at customs on many occasions and being asked if I was a vendor or worse, a supplier of soft porn. Luckily, I had some photographs and interviews in my press kit to prove that I was a popular film star back in India. I would be let off with a disbelieving nod.

Not too many Indians lived in Beverly Hills back then. Among those who did were scientist and studio-owner Raj Dutt and his wife Kumkum, my extended family in LA who made me feel I was one of their own. They were Bengalis from Kolkata who had made it big in the US. Then of course there was Bikram Choudhury and his wife, Rajashree. Bikram dada is the founder of Bikram Yoga which had become very popular with the hip and happening crowd. He lived in a palatial mansion, had several Rolls-Royces, and was a fabulous host. He opened his home and heart to me. Bikram dada also introduced me to Iqbal Qasim, a well-known businessman, and his wife Yasmin bhabhi, who too were a great help.

Film-maker V. Shantaram-ji's daughter, Rajshree, was another Indian who had made it in the US. While shooting with Raj Kapoor for *Around the World* in the US, she had met an American student, Greg Chapman, married him three years later, and moved to LA permanently. She runs a custom-made clothing business with her husband. Another actress who had settled down in West Hollywood was director Kedar Kapoor's daughter Madhu Kapoor who had worked in films like *Manokaamnaa* and *Siskiyan*. Her warmth and support steadied me in an alien land.

Those from the Indian media who supported me in every way imaginable were Ramesh Morarka and his wife Beena, publisher and owner of the newspaper *India-West*, and Reshma Dordi, the only Indian host of a TV show in the West at the time, *Showbiz India*.

There were a few other Indians I remember from the time, such as plastic surgeon Dr Raj Kanodia and Babu Subramaniam who worked with Mahesh Bhatt saab in films like *Lahu Ke Do Rang*, Kabir Bedi in *Sandokan* and *Black Pirate* and was one of the most sought-after first assistant directors in Hollywood.

Omnipresent in this crowd was Jagmohan Mundhra, the Indian-American director, producer and screenwriter of films like *Kamla, Night Eyes* and *L.A. Goddess*. Jagmohan-ji's house was often referred to as 'India House' because any visitor from India, be it Rekha-ji, Shabana Azmi-ji or Sushmita Sen was his guest. He was a dear friend with whom I later collaborated on *Bawandar, Backwaters, Monsoon* and *Shoot on Sight*. He passed away too soon, at the age of sixty-two from pneumonia and multiple organ failure.

His film *Shoot on Sight* gave me the rare opportunity of acting alongside Naseeruddin Shah and Om Puri, that too for a month at a stretch. Om Puri had been my teacher at acting school while I had met Naseer bhai at the FTII and acted with him in *Hum Paanch*. Interestingly, my role was switched with Om-ji's just a few days before filming began. I was to play the antagonist and Om-ji and Naseer bhai were best friends. Suddenly I got a call from Jagmohan-ji saying that Naseer felt the roles should be switched as Om-ji and he had played friends in many films. I agreed with some trepidation and I am glad I did. Thrown in with these two powerhouse performers, my performance benefitted immensely.

All these wonderful friends contributed tremendously to my Hollywood journey. I stayed in their homes, they would cook hot meals for me and set up meetings with film-makers. They even took turns ferrying me around depending on who was free. There was no Uber cab service back then, and since I don't drive, I had to rely on my friends, their friends and their kids to drop me off and pick me up from appointments.

In those early years of trying my luck in Hollywood, I had the honour of being invited to be the grand marshal at the Los Angeles India Day parade by my friend, A.J. Dudheker. Seeing so many happy Indians in LA, celebrating India which was miles away from home, reinforced my determination to make it in Hollywood.

On another occasion, I had the opportunity to be co-grand marshal, along with Rani Mukerji at the India Day parade in New York, thanks to my friend Bipin Patel. I will never forget the sight of the Empire State Building lit up in the Indian tricolour. I also developed a deep connection with the Fog Festival in San Francisco and its driving force, Dr Romesh Japra. The cardiologist and I share a relationship rooted in our respect for the arts. I have loved being a part of the Fog Festival and the India Day parade in San Francisco.

Years later, I made the acquaintance of producer Raju Patel and his wife Dimple who also lived in Beverly Hills and were very welcoming. Raju had grown up in Kenya and the UK; I introduced him to the vibrant Indian community there who had adopted me as a representative of their country and its cinema.

Despite their help and warmth, there were times when I wondered what I was doing in a city that treated me like a rank newcomer while the biggest film industry in the world was waiting to put their favourite 'Bad Man' in front of the camera. In India, a billion fans crowded the theatres every time one of my films released to whistle at my entry and cheer at my dialogues.

One of the popular Indian restaurants in the US at the time was Bombay Palace and every Indian who came to LA could be found there. Shekhar was one of the regulars. I also spotted Vijay and Ashok Amritraj, tennis aces who had successfully entered the entertainment field. I tried many times then to meet the brothers, but failed. Years later, Ashok became a very good friend. Today, he is one of my strongest supporters in Hollywood. I was a special guest at his book release. The owner of the restaurant, Deep Singh, and his wife went out of their way to introduce me to bigwigs in the American film industry who they thought could help me, apart from providing me the comfort of home-cooked meals.

My LA journey would not be complete without a mention of my friend, Ash Gupta, an Indian-born internationally known photographer whose portfolio includes Ben Affleck, Jennifer Lawrence, Steven Seagal, Carmen Electra to name a few. Whenever I am in the city of angels, I hang out with Ash and his family and his picture-perfect art never fails to bedazzle me. He has also been a guardian for my son Sanjay in LA, apart from the Dutts, whose home in LA became my home away from home.

There were producers waiting in queue for me, calling and entreating me to return home. I knew the instant I got back to Mumbai, I could sign twenty Hindi films. But something kept me back in LA. There were many frustrating days and sleepless nights when I would wonder if it was a self-destructive move or if I could really be a trailblazer for my country and its fraternity. But there was one thing I learnt and learnt well: not to give up without a fight. And so, I stayed on . . .

14

HOW THE WEST WAS WON

After *The Second Jungle Book: Mowgli & Baloo*, I got several offers one of which was for a series along the same lines by 20th Century Fox. Its action director, Solly Marx, and animal trainer, Brian McMillan, who had worked with me in *The Second Jungle Book*, spoke about me strongly to the studio, insisting that I was well suited for the role. But I had to turn down the series because I couldn't stay nine months in Costa Rica. That would derail the films I was working on back home, I told the studio executives who were keen to have me on board.

20th Century Fox was ready to compromise and give me a break for a couple of weeks during the shoot to fly down to India and wrap up my assignments. They didn't understand when I told them that it was not enough time as I had multiple films on the floor. In Hollywood, they work only on one project at a time and the film-makers couldn't imagine me playing a robber in the morning and a cop later in the day. But that's how Bollywood works. Some actors work three shifts a day, juggle six or more films at a time, month after month, and still deliver wonderful performances. That's the magic of Bollywood!

I had also been approached for a Disney film, *Eddie*, with Whoopi Goldberg playing a rabid basketball fan, Edwina 'Eddie' Franklin, who attends every game to root for her team. The film had an African-American casting director, Robert Cannon, who offered me a role. He reasoned that since Whoopi improvised a lot on the sets and I had years of experience, I wouldn't be thrown by her and so was the best candidate for the job.

I was happy with the offer until I was given my scenes. I realized then that my character had zero IQ. He was unable to recognize a landmark as familiar as the Empire State Building when he was parked right in front of it till Eddie points it out to him. Worse, I was expected to speak with an atrocious English accent. Not wanting to misrepresent my countrymen, many of whom are suave, intelligent and speak impeccable English, I turned down the offer. This angered my agent who told me that I could be a big fish in a tank called Bollywood, but this was Hollywood that drew talent from every corner of the globe. He was so angry that he refused to even meet me and just told me to pick up my photographs from the reception because he no longer wanted to represent me.

I was in the running for another comedy, *Dear God*, a sweet little film about a mother telling her kids that when faced with difficulties, they should simply write to God and He would solve all their problems. The letters, addressed to God, end up at the post office where the hero, played by Greg Kinnear, starts to read and answer them. Once his secret is out, he is dragged to court because in the US it is a crime to open someone else's mail without his or her consent. I was offered the role of the head postmaster, a highly qualified gentleman who for want of a better opportunity ends up at the post office and comes to the hero's rescue. It was an interesting, positive role, but not what I wanted for my second film. I turned it down as well and it was goodbye to the second agent.

Then, just when everyone was getting ready to write me off, I was signed for a big film featuring Sean Connery. The contract was drawn up and mailed to my new agents, Jim Cota and

Michael Livingston. The studio, 20th Century Fox again, was offering $100,000 less than what my agents were expecting and so we went back and forth about the money. I tried to persuade my agents to let me accept the film at the fee they were offering because it was the kind of Hollywood break I had been hoping for. They waved me off, saying confidently, 'Gulshan, we have the deal all sewn up. You go enjoy a nice dinner tonight, tomorrow, when you come to the office, we will have the contract in the bag.' The next day I learnt that Naseeruddin Shah was in and I was out. The film was Stephen Norrington's *The League of Extraordinary Gentleman*, which was set in the Victorian era and revolved around a secret mission.

I befriended many producers and directors in LA. I continued to carry DVDs of Hindi films in my suitcase and would arrange private screenings for them. A few film-makers saw them and raved about the exotic locations, the beautiful Indian girls with their kohl-lined eyes, including the background dancers. They had expected the actors to be traditionally dressed in a dhoti or pyjama-kurta and were pleasantly surprised to see them smartly turned out in Western wear. Only the frequent song-and-dance routines left them bemused till I explained that through these songs we expressed our emotions and took the story forward.

The exposure to Indian cinema helped change certain perceptions, one of them being that Indians spoke English with a strange accent. I acknowledged that we did have an exaggerated way of delivering our lines onscreen, a few decibels too loud at times and with a lot of gesticulation, but that was to compensate for the poor infrastructure of our theatres. The sound projectors in some of the theatres in the smaller towns were in terrible condition, so as the 'Bad Man', I would hold what was usually a cordless phone in my hand and say menacingly, 'If I press this button (*pointing to it*) on the remote here, the bomb there (*pointing in the other direction*) will go off.'

This way, even if the lines were inaudible, viewers would understand what was being said.

Meanwhile, I continued to live and work back home, the first Indian actor to do so. But I would frequently dash off across the Atlantic, and with each trip I was bridging the gap between the two countries and their film industries and becoming a familiar face in Beverley Hills in the process. Actors and film-makers started warming up to me even though they were still clueless about our country because there was no Google then to educate them on India, our cinema and its stars. When war broke out in Afghanistan or there was a shootout in Kashmir, they would call me with genuine concern to ask if my family was fine. I had to explain that despite our proximity to Afghanistan on the map, it was another country, while Kashmir was another state in India, miles away from Maharashtra where I lived. In the pre-Internet era, I became a brand ambassador for both India and Bollywood.

Breaking into Hollywood was a far more difficult journey than my initial struggles in Mumbai. In 2000, I was introduced to Goldie Hawn by a friend and she instantly invited me to dinner at her residence. At the time, I was shooting for an American sci-fi horror film, *Tail Sting*. Excitedly, I told the director, Paul Wynne, and the director of photography, Angel Colmenares, that I would have to leave by a certain time that evening as I was Goldie's guest. Morris Ruskin, the producer, offered to drop me, but by the time we had packed-up and were on our way, it was almost 7 p.m. Goldie's other guests were getting hungry and I started getting frantic calls enquiring about my whereabouts. By the time I arrived at her home, everyone was seated around a large table outside, waiting to start dinner.

There was Goldie's beau, Kurt Russell, her friend and legendary actress Susan Sarandon, along with a director and a producer whose names I don't remember. They proudly informed me that they had got Indian food and soon we were digging into butter chicken and kebabs, and chatting about shoots. Being a comedienne, I had expected Goldie to be funny, but Susan, an Academy Award winner, turned out to be even more hilarious, imitating an Italian director she had worked with to the smallest detail. It was an enjoyable and memorable evening.

I can't say the same about my encounter with Bruce Willis. I had been invited to the premiere of the crime comedy-drama *Bandits*. It was a full house and among the guests were MGM's Michael Nathanson, Bob Levin and Erik Lomis, producers Ashok Amritraj, David Hoberman, Michael Birnbaum and Arnold Rifkin, the film's star Bruce Willis with his children and ex-wife Demi Moore, and actor, film-maker, singer, musician Billy Bob Thornton. I also met Michael Ovitz, Wesley Snipes, Michael Bay, Halle Berry, Sandy Climan, Bob Cooper, Julie Delpy, Samuel L. Jackson, Brad Krevoy and Matthew Perry to name a few. The who's who of Hollywood was there, at the premiere and at the after-party at Spago, LA's most exclusive restaurant, where I bumped into the charming Angelina Jolie who was very cordial. Years later, she would come to India with then husband Brad Pitt to shoot their home production, *A Mighty Heart*.

A journalist of Tibetan origin, Liza Sering, was covering the event. She was excited to see an Indian star at an A-list Hollywood party and asked me who all I had met and my views about Hollywood stars. Bruce Willis's name came up during the conversation. When I told her that I had not met him yet, she took me along with her and introduced us. He was cold and dismissive and his behaviour stung. However, Richard Gere, a big star after *Pretty Woman*, and Steven Seagal, Goldie Hawn, Salma Hayek, Al Pacino and Arnold Schwarzenegger were happy to learn that a successful Indian actor had come to Hollywood to explore new horizons.

Soon after, my friend Madhu Kapoor set up a meeting with Steven Seagal. On the appointed day, we arrived at his house, which had many dangerous-looking dogs growling at you and several Buddhist flags fluttering outside. We were ushered into the living room where, as we waited for Steven, I noticed a lot of activity in the kitchen. People were talking loudly, gesturing towards me, walking in and out of the living room, and giving me the 'look'. At first, I assumed that all these associates of Steven were Spanish, but I quickly realized that many were from Tibet, Nepal and other neighbouring countries of India. I figured that they were my fans and soon they were requesting me not to leave without taking a few photographs with them. It amused me that in the home of a Hollywood superstar there were people dying to get photographed with me.

When Steven appeared, my admirers melted away. He was warm and asked in Hindi, 'India *mein sab theek hai?*' He then enquired about my work and admitted that he was familiar with some of my films. 'You are an incredible actor. I want to take you in one of my films as a strong antagonist,' he asserted. My day was made!

Meanwhile, the clatter in the kitchen had escalated. Being a star, I knew this was my fans' way of telling me not to leave without giving them photographs and autographs. I asked Steven if he would mind if I posed for some pictures with some of his associates. He was surprised by my request but magnanimously called everyone into the living room for an impromptu photo shoot.

A few months later, we met in New York at a beauty pageant and charity event where Steven was the chief guest. He was delighted to see me and told me we should grab dinner. I happily accepted his invitation and went to sit at my table. When it was time to leave, he walked up to me with his entourage and said, 'Come along, brother.' Steven is always in the company of several pretty girls. He had also invited the girl who had just been crowned and they all got in as his limousine pulled up. I was waiting to follow them when his secretary stopped me, saying, 'Sir, you can drive in the car behind.'

I snarled back, 'What's wrong with this one? I'm getting into this car, any problem?'

Steven, who was already inside with the girls, said, 'What happened, brother? Get in.'

I ducked in, with one last glare at his secretary.

We went to a Tibetan restaurant called Tsampa, tucked along the 9th Street corridor of the Japanese row, and all hell broke loose! Steven, a practising Buddhist, was a frequent visitor at Tsampa, as were several Hollywood stars, but they had never had a Bollywood actor coming there to dine before. Chefs came running out of the kitchen and guests from their tables came to ours, along with the waiters and the manager. Steven knew I was a star like him back home but was still baffled by their interest, and asked me curiously, 'What did you do, brother?' I laughed and told him that all these people wanted photographs with me.

The staff who had ended their shift and left by the time we reached, got calls alerting them about our presence. They told their co-workers not to let me go till they returned. They caught trains, buses and even cabs and came back to the restaurant with their friends and families for autographs and photographs. Even the owner, an old friend of Steven's, was there. 'Jhumpa, what are you doing here?' he asked the elderly gentleman in Tibetan, as he bowed low in the traditional Buddhist greeting. The man bowed back and after an exchange of greetings told him, 'Rinpoche, I had reached home and was sleeping when I got a call telling me that Gulshan Grover was here, so I returned.' Meanwhile, his colleagues were requesting me to pose with them and I was only too happy to oblige. I like to end my meal with a dessert. That evening, when I asked for something meetha, six varieties of sweets were laid out for me. Even as I was digging into them, I knew that I owed this sweetness to the popularity of Bollywood movies and its stars across the globe. I thank you, Steven, for graciously allowing me to enjoy that moment of glory.

The evening was a revelation to Steven. New York is his city. He is the superstar there who can't step out without security, and so he usually whizzes about in limousines and flies in private jets. I did not have such luxuries, but my popularity matched his and other Hollywood stars' in a country that is not my own. The evening was also a revelation for me. I knew this had nothing to do with me or any other actor per se—it was Bollywood, long maligned by critics and agents, that has given us our identity and our mass following. I felt honoured to be a part of it.

Incidents like this continued to surprise me, giving me some of the biggest highs of my life. When I reflect on them, I realize they not only boosted my morale but also the stature of the industry I had come across the world to promote. It reaffirmed the power of commercial Hindi films and made me proud that our cinema stood tall in Hollywood.

Soon after, Steven came to India. My close friend Vikas Verma, who runs a security company and was in charge of Steven's security, informed me that Steven wanted to meet me. Needless to say, I went to the Taj Mahal Palace Hotel where he was staying. The three of us were sitting in the hotel, when Steven, who had been cooped up indoors meeting people all day, suddenly jumped up, saying he wanted to step out for a breath of fresh air. 'Let's take a walk outside, brother,' he said, turning to me.

I was hesitant. 'Walk outside the Taj? I'm not sure that's a good idea,' I demurred.

But Steven was not to be stopped. 'Why, brother? I have security, come along,' he urged, looking at Vikas, who nodded in agreement.

I was still doubtful. 'I really don't think that's a good idea,' I said. But with a 'Nah, nah, nothing is going to happen,' he swept me out. Steven, his security entourage, Vikas and I stepped out of the hotel, crossed the road to the Gateway of India, and pandemonium broke out!

My fans had spotted me and with a roar of '*Dekho*, Gulshan Grover,' they swooped down on me. Steven is a phenomenon, and many would recognize him in India, but I was the 'Bad Man' here and in their excitement to reach me, even he was shoved aside. Finally, his bodyguards had to rescue not just him, but me too from the mob frenzy.

All this happened over a decade ago, and slowly my name began to resonate in the West too among Hollywood actors and technicians. When they asked about me, they realized I was a household name in my country. One director of photography went to an Indian restaurant in LA and wondered if they had heard of an actor called Gulshan Grover. Right from the chef to the proprietor, everyone came rushing out to 'see' me. 'Where is he?' they asked him, and when he informed them that he had been shooting with me, he was told to bring me along next time. 'The meal is on us,' they promised him and next morning, he narrated the incident to me with new respect in his eyes, saying reverentially, 'Hey man, you sure are one popular actor!'

I had seen the same reaction at Flavor of India, a restaurant in LA, where actors like Keanu Reeves ate undisturbed. But my visit there triggered a tsunami of sorts. I remain eternally grateful to the wonderful Indians who live outside India but embrace me with so much warmth. They are a noisy, vibrant bunch, the girls screaming, 'Oh my God, oh my God, it's Gulshan! Can I hug you, please!' OMG, they always make me feel special!

On one occasion, I had accompanied a doctor friend to a famous Chinese restaurant in Beverly Hills. Stevie Wonder and his friends were sitting at a table. Someone pointed me out to him, saying I was a famous Bollywood actor, and the famous singer and musician graciously walked up to me with his associates to say that he loved our music and would love to collaborate with an Indian someday. He was very warm and invited me to join him at his table so we could carry on with our conversation. Miles away from home, Stevie Wonder made me feel like I belonged and that I wasn't just an unwanted stranger.

Perceptions were changing back home as well. When I was shooting with Amitabh Bachchan-ji on the sets of Veeru Devgan-ji's patriotic drama, *Hindustan Ki Kasam*, he would often ask me between shots how it was like working in LA and I would reply, 'I love it, sir, you should also work there.' Amit-ji would smile and say, 'Someone should sign me for a Hollywood film first before that can happen.' Amitabh Bachchan is humility personified! Veeru-ji also wanted to film a mid-air action sequence in Hollywood and I arranged for the action coordinators, the location and permissions to make his dream possible.

Queenie Singh, the jewellery designer, believed there was a market for her exotic pieces in the West but didn't know how to go about it. She came to me for advice, as did several Bollywood actresses with queries about how to find an agent in LA, put together a showreel and ace an audition. I was happy to help in any way I could.

During the filming of his official Indian adaptation of the American TV series, *24,* even Anil Kapoor sought me out given my years of experience in Hollywood. We were staying at Regent Beverly Wilshire, the hotel where *Pretty Woman* was filmed. Every evening after pack-up, Anil and I would meet for dinner and he would take my advice and guidance on a variety of subjects, from agents and publicists to the shoot and offers he was getting. Incidentally, I had been offered a role in Danny Boyle's drama *Slumdog Millionaire*, that of the police inspector. But the film was shot in India, and I had another commitment that took me away. The role went to Irrfan Khan. When I saw Anil and Irrfan with Freida Pinto, Dev Patel and the kids walking the red carpet at the

Oscars, I told myself, 'Hey, Gulshan, you could have been out there too in a sexy suit.' I wish I could have done that film.

Meanwhile, back in India, I received a bizarre request from the son of a legendary actor who told me that he was all set to sign Sanjay Dutt for his next film. 'But I just read that Pierce Brosnan has announced that he is not going to play James Bond any more. That means he's free. If he agrees, I could replace Sanjay with Pierce in my film. Why don't you ask him if he is interested?' he told me. Usually, I have an answer to everything, but this one time I was left speechless!

I couldn't bring Bond down for a Hindi movie, but I did manage, in some way, to cement a bond between Bollywood and Hollywood over the span of a decade through constant discussions about our cinema. Today, it feels good when I am introduced to Mel Gibson and the 'Braveheart' smiles and says, 'I have seen your work. India is a wonderful country.' There was a time when Hollywood publicists would pass these stars slips of paper with some of our big names, such as Amitabh Bachchan, Shah Rukh Khan and Aishwarya Rai Bachchan, so that they could bring them up in conversation. It's a common publicity plot. Even when I was in Spain for the India International Film Awards (IIFA)—which showcases Indian cinema, taking its fragrance to new destinations, thanks to the efforts of my friends and hosts, the supremely talented Andre Timmins, Viraf Sarkari and Sabbas Joseph—I made it a point to mention Javier Bardem, their most popular local star and an Oscar winner, in my interviews. In Paris, I would bring up Jean Reno, the French actor who made a name internationally with *Mission: Impossible*, *Godzilla* and *The Da Vinci Code* in the course of my interviews.

My first visit to the French Riviera was almost a quarter of a century ago. No significant Bollywood actor had been to the prestigious Cannes Film Festival before. There was just one Indian stall at the 'market' where I hung out with the chairman of the

National Film Development Corporation (NFDC) and Jagmohan Mundhra-ji during the day. The evening galas and cocktails came later. Back then, there was only one Indian restaurant in Cannes and many of the tables there were booked by the NFDC. I was among their select guests. There was also the customary dinner hosted by the Hindujas at their villa and I can never forget their warmth and the personal care and affection they bestowed on me. Today, I am proud to see Indian actresses like Priyanka Chopra, Aishwarya Rai Bachchan, Deepika Padukone, Kangana Ranaut and Sonam Kapoor to name a few walking the Cannes red carpet. I am proud to see Vidya Balan and Nandita Das as a part of the esteemed Cannes jury. And I am proud that Indian cinema has come a long way since then.

Today, it's not that difficult to get a shot at Hollywood as India is seen as an economically vibrant country that has stood strong in the face of worldwide recession. Indian actors are valued because their presence in a Hollywood film translates into better viewership and more business. We, the stars of commercial Hindi cinema, were once ridiculed for our over-the-top performances and our songs and dances. Now, we are lauded for our star power and realistic portrayals, and much sought after. My victory came not from romancing Julia Roberts or working in a Steven Spielberg film, but from proving that given a chance, we can be the best of the best.

I was able to make inroads into Hollywood by exposing them to our Bollywood platter, which left them with a taste for the exotic. No longer is our cinema considered unpalatable or our stars temperamental. Never mind the two-hour run-time and lack of subtitles, at least I introduced the West to the talent in the world's largest film-making industry, thus making it easier for those who crossed over in the future.

Of course, it came at a price. But here too I had producer friends like Rahul Mittra to offer a helping hand. Rahul understood that due to my long stints in Hollywood, my visibility in Indian cinema had reduced considerably and I was looking to return with a bang. Reading my mind, he convinced Tigmanshu Dhulia to cast me as the villain in *Bullet Raja*, which gave me a chance to shine again. Later, Rahul introduced me to a crusader and supporter of the Sikh community, Raju Chadha-ji. What I admire about Raju-ji is that he not only takes a strong stand on social issues, he doesn't shy away from financially supporting these causes. He is also a producer of note and the chairman of Wave Cinemas and his support has been invaluable.

Rahul, Tigmanshu and Sanjay Dutt later collaborated on *Sahib Biwi Aur Gangster 3*. Many years ago, through Sanju I had met Bala. B. Balaji Rao is the managing director of Venky's Chicken and has contributed to the overall growth of the poultry industry in India. We were introduced at the launch of Anubhav Sinha's spy thriller *Dus*. The dashing businessman was surrounded by foreign security guards and commandoes and I admit I was somewhat intimidated by him at the time. But I met him again with Sanju at his home in Pune and that's where I discovered what a warm person Bala is. Our mutual admiration society keeps the bond strong.

Today, with big-ticket movies like *Sooryavanshi*, *Sadak 2* and *Mumbai Saga*, 'Bad Man' is back in the race. But what is more heartening is that after me, my son carried on with the effort of building a mud path between two different cinemas and two of the biggest film industries in the world, screening Indian films at MGM's office in Beverly Hills during his tenure there and creating a number of joint ventures and co-production deals between Bollywood and Hollywood.

And the journey did not end there. It continued into other cinemas, other worlds . . .

15

THE WORLD AND ME

Sitting in snow-clad Warsaw, I felt privileged to be the first Indian actor to be working in a Polish film. This was the country of Roman Polanski, Jerzy Kawalerowicz, Andrzej Munk and Andrzej Wajda. This was the country of Agnieszka Holland, Krzysztof Kieślowski, Wojciech Marczewski and Krzysztof Zanussi. This was the country of priceless gems like Polanski's debut film *Knife in the Water*, which bagged him an Oscar nomination. Forty years later, he took home the coveted trophy for best director for *The Pianist*.

My Polish production *Nie Means Nie* (*No Means No*) was a pioneering effort to bring together the talents of two very different film-making countries. Sanjay got me this role believing that being a single father myself, I would empathize with my character. And it was Vikas Verma who made it happen.

A year earlier, I had started filming *I'm Not a Terrorist*, becoming the first Indian actor to act in a Malaysian film. The Minister of Tourism and Culture, Dato' Seri Mohamed Nazri Abdul Aziz, who likes my work, came for the trailer and poster launch in Petaling Jaya, Selangor, straight from parliament. It gave me immense satisfaction to be representing my country and film industry in another part of the world.

When Norwegian prime minister Erna Solberg opened the film festival in Oslo, an Iranian delegation, headed by writer

and director Ghorban Mohammadpour, was also present
at the occasion. After the prime minister had felicitated me,
Ghorban—who has made path-breaking films like *Women Are
Angels*, *Fasele* and *Zaban Madari*—approached me through my
friend Nasreen Qureshi to work in one of his films and gave
me the script. And I became the first Indian actor to act in an
Iranian film.

I lived most of 2015 out of a suitcase, spending a white
Christmas on the sets of a German film. I also worked on another
German–French film, *Rose and Marguerite*, in which I played a
rebel chief. At first, I was a bit sceptical because I can't speak
either German or French, but the film-makers reassured me that if
it got too difficult, I could say my lines in English. I turned up in a
kurta-pyjama for the first meet-and-greet session with the cast and
crew, and our dashing German leading man Ralf Bauer took one
look at me and quipped, 'Hey, he should be playing the prince,
not me. He looks tailor-made for the role!' That was so gracious
of my friend, Ralf.

Working with a multinational crew was a huge learning
experience. The only thing I missed was the mirror. In India,
every Bollywood actor will look into a mirror before a shot, but
in the West, you have a make-up man or woman observing you
from a distance. If something needs fixing, they will hurry across
for a quick touch-up. My make-up woman did not even carry a
mirror in her bag, and it rattled me that there were no mirrors
in the forest where we were shooting because I needed to see
for myself to ensure that my hair and make-up was all right, a
Bollywood habit hard to break. One day, the producer arrived at
the location and announced that he had a gift for me. Everyone
crowded around me as I unwrapped it. He had got me a mirror
all the way from Paris.

Another exciting collaboration was *Prisoners of the Sun*, a
British–French horror adventure that brought together actors

from Britain, Wales, France and Canada. There was John Rhys-Davies, the Welsh actor who played Gimli in *The Lord of the Rings* trilogy, and Sallah, the excavator of the *Indiana Jones* franchise. French actor, model and singer David Franck Charvet, popular as Matt Brody in the television series *Baywatch*, and Nick Moran, the English actor, writer, producer, director, best known as Eddy the card sharp in Guy Ritchie's *Lock, Stock and Two Smoking Barrels*, and Scabior in *Harry Potter and the Deathly Hallows—Part 1 and 2*—were also on board, as was Emily Holmes, the Canadian actress who appeared on television in *Night Visions* and *Dark Angel*. The British–French actress, director and granddaughter of Charlie Chaplin, Carmen Chaplin, was also a part of the cast, and I had many interesting conversations with her about her legendary grandfather who, without uttering a word, could make us laugh and cry.

Prisoners of the Sun was about an expedition in the deserts of Egypt to discover a secret older than time and more dangerous than death. I joined the shoot a little late and everyone was eagerly waiting to meet Professor Rohit Singh. One day, while they were all at the bar, I strode in for my introduction scene, surprised to find every pair of eyes fixed unblinkingly on me. Slightly discomfited by the attention, I asked, 'Is anything the matter? Do I owe someone money?' They laughed and shook their heads admitting that they had been expecting an elderly Indian gentleman and not someone so young and dashing.

The film was shot in Ouarzazate in Morocco, which had earlier played host to big Hollywood units like *Gladiator*. We stayed for a month in a seven-star hotel with film memorabilia displayed in beautiful glass cases in the lobby. The only thing I really missed was my daal as there was not a single Indian restaurant in the vicinity. On my way to the shoot, I arrived at the Casablanca international airport to learn that the flight to Ouarzazate was scheduled to take off seven hours later.

However, the lady immigration officer looked at me and shook her head, 'No visa for you.'

Intrigued, I asked, 'Why not?'

She retorted, 'Because you beat up Shah Rukh Khan.'

I was momentarily confused, before realizing that she was talking about our movies. It turned out that she and the other women immigration officers were die-hard SRK fans. I promised not to bash up Shah Rukh ever again and even bring him along with me during my next visit so they could all get his autograph personally. How could I explain that what they saw onscreen was all playacting and that I was actually indebted to SRK for kick-starting my career in world cinema.

I quickly learnt that even though we were working towards creating interesting cinema, no two film units were the same anywhere in the world. In Hollywood, smoking on the sets is prohibited. Even on an outdoor shoot, in the middle of nowhere, you cannot light up. There are special smoking zones created for you to enjoy a smoke if you must. At the other end of the scale are the French. The director of photography will have a cigarette dangling from his lips, as will every second person on the set. In India, if you are seen with a glass in your hand, you are branded an alcoholic, while in France it's not unusual to have a glass of wine in your hand or a bottle of beer when you are at work.

My international projects took me to Canada and into writer, director and producer R. Paul Dhillon's romcom *The Fusion Generation*. The film had several Canadian actors, including Sitara Hewitt, the star of the TV series *Little Mosque on the Prairie*. I played an Indo-Canadian lumber mogul in this fun-filled journey through the Punjabi community's rich history in British Columbia.

However, Canada for me is intrinsically associated with Deepa Mehta. As I had mentioned in an earlier chapter, I was one of the first actors to be confirmed for Deepa's *Fire* and had even started working on my 'look' when I was inexplicably dropped from the film. Being stupidly angry with what had happened in the past, I had stopped communicating with Deepa.

It was while I was shooting *Mr & Mrs Khiladi* in Toronto with Akshay Kumar that Deepa asked me if I'd be interested in the role of a Sardar in her Partition drama *1947: Earth*. It was the second instalment in her Elements trilogy. I didn't even go through the script because I was still angry with her. Deepa sent me a couple of faxes and emails that I didn't bother to answer.

Then, I got a call from Aamir Khan who was playing Dil Nawaz, the Ice-Candy Man, who, along with Hassan the masseur (Rahul Khanna), is in love with Nandita Das's Shanta, the little girl's ayah and the film's narrator. Aamir called me twice, wondering what I thought of the script. I admitted that I had junked it and explained why. Being a sensitive actor who might have gone through a similar situation himself, Aamir insisted that I forget the past and do the film. It was hard to turn away Aamir. He has been a friend since we worked together in B. Subhash's *Love Love Love*. I respect him, and on his request, I agreed to read the script. It was sent to me again and after going through it, I relented and gave dates for *1947: Earth*. Unfortunately, they clashed with those I had allotted for the climax of *Hindustan Ki Kasam*. Aamir spoke to the film's producer, Jhamu Sugandh, and his brother Harish, and they agreed to relieve me.

I took a flight to Delhi and drove straight to Deepa's house for dinner and a workshop with the rest of the team. I was still simmering when I turned up on the set. After the first few shots, Deepa put her arm around my shoulders and took me for a long walk. I don't know what guru mantra she chanted, but it cleansed away all the anger. We returned and I gave a perfect take. After the film's release, Naseer called to say, 'Gulshan Grover, you were the best!' This rare good man's role also brought compliments from Om Puri saab, Anil Kapoor and Aamir himself. I give all credit to Deepa for getting that performance out of a reluctant actor.

She is one of the best directors I have worked with, and *1947: Earth* remains one of my personal favourites—a film I am truly proud of.

I played a Sardar again in Deepa's crime thriller *Beeba Boys*. Robbie Grewal is a mafia don who runs his business like a serious enterprise till the Beeba boys, with their fast cars, fashionable suits and lust for power, challenge his authority. Then, the 'Bad Man' gets into action. What made Robbie distinctive was that deep down he remains a good family man who, between dealing drugs and gunning down people, plays golf, frequents religious places and spends time with his wife and daughter. Deepa wanted us to bond like a real family. So, every evening after pack-up, I would pick up Monica Deol, who played my wife (she was Canada's first MTV VJ), and Gia Sandhu, who played my daughter, whom I fondly called Chhoti, and head to the best restaurants. It was an 'assignment' paid for by production, and though I usually like to hole up in my room after pack-up, going over the next day's scenes, I came to enjoy these 'family' dinners in Toronto. For Monica and the other Indian–Canadian actors on the film, as also the Sardarji who tied my turban for every take, I was a Bollywood matinee idol and they knew every dialogue of mine, from *Ram Lakhan* to *Raja Ki Aayegi Baraat*.

Deepa is always warm with her actors and pampers them to give their best, but she is the boss on the set. She knows exactly what she wants, believes you can give it to her, and if you don't deliver, tears you to pieces. *Beeba Boys* was her first action film, and only once did I do something that was not in sync with the character while we were filming a scene. That evening, I received a four-page email from a very upset Deepa telling me that I had deviated from her brief. Chastised, the next day I made sure that I did not give her any reason to complain again. After pack-up, as the car drew to a stop outside my hotel, the phone rang. It was her assistant, informing me that Deepa would be picking me up at the hotel in an hour. As I showered and got ready, I wondered what I had done to upset her again. As she was ordering drinks and dinner, I waited for the axe to fall. But it didn't. Instead, my beaming director told me how happy she was with my performance and that's why she was treating me to dinner. The breath left me in a rush.

The four-page emails continued with Deepa outlining her brief to the minutest detail. If I measured up, I got taken out for a drink. *Beeba* means 'good' in Punjabi. Her *beeba* boy was Randeep Hooda while I was her *beeba* friend. The film premiered at the Toronto International Film Festival on 13 September 2015. This once, thirteen wasn't an unlucky number.

The same year, a month later, on 7 October, the Australian rom-com *UnIndian* premiered in Sydney where it had been shot. It featured Aussie cricketer Brett Lee in the lead opposite Tannishtha Chatterjee, playing an attractive divorcee and single mother, Meera. I was Deepak Khurana, Meera's ex-husband, who is intent on whisking off their daughter, Smitha, to India because he loves her. The film was funded by the Australia India Film Fund and had a predominantly local cast and crew. Brett Lee, a wonderful guy and a great entertainer on the set, admitted that they had expected me to turn down the film.

I also worked on the Canadian film *The Flight*, in which I played a single parent who wants his only son to take over his business empire. The problem is that the boy wants to be a musician. This leads to him being ousted from the family home.

Closer home, I was part of another international film, *We're No Monks*. Written and directed by Pema Dhondup, it was about four confused and disillusioned Tibetans exiled in Dharamshala. Pema, who has studied film-making at the University of Southern California (USC) on a Fulbright scholarship, sent me an email telling me about the film and wondering if I would accept the lead role of a police officer in McLeod Ganj who starts out intensely disliking these four boys as he believes they don't belong there, but ends up helping them. I was happy to jump on board.

Since he had a paltry budget, many of us, including me, worked for free. I even borrowed a cop's uniform from another film's wardrobe and arrived without a make-up man or a hairdresser. A young Tibetan girl did the make-up for all of us, and to Pema's amazed delight, I even stayed in a small hotel with the rest of the unit so as not to make a big hole in his production costs. I suffered the biting cold for my love of cinema.

My dear friend wanted to shoot on the streets and in the market with real crowds, even filming the Dalai Lama's convoy as it went past. Thanks to my amazing popularity in Dharamshala and McLeod Ganj, crowds weren't a problem. Wherever I went, hordes of fans would gather to see the 'Bad Man' and even the lathi-wielding cops couldn't wrestle them away.

As a bonus I got to meet His Holiness, the Dalai Lama. What a moment it was to be blessed by him! And how humble of His Holiness to thank me for being a part of this film with his countrymen.

I also collaborated with Pema on an American–English film called *The Man from Kathmandu*, which had a stellar international cast. He had sent me the script, telling me to take my pick. I chose the role of the antagonist and flew to freezing Kathmandu for the shoot. The warmth of my fans melted away all traces of physical discomfort. I had last visited Nepal when my friend Manisha Koirala had got married. She had acquainted me with Nepali culture, its tradition, language and cuisine. As soon as I reached Kathmandu, I went for a costume trial. Dressed up in traditional Nepalese attire, complete with the topi, I got myself photographed. I wrote in Nepali, 'Manisha, I am here in Nepal for you' and shared the picture with her. She instantly welcomed me to her country, posting the picture on Instagram. Later, she visited me on the set and took me out. I went to her house with the team for a Nepalese dinner as well.

After I completed the film, I zipped back to Warsaw. The director of *Nie Means Nie* had been waiting anxiously for a carpet of snow for weeks. One of the effects of climate change was that Poland did not get much snow even in December that year and as a result, shooting had been delayed. Eventually the weather obliged and from the biting cold of Kathmandu, I embraced a white and wintery Warsaw with the same burning passion that had brought me from Delhi to Mumbai all those years ago and driven me to chase my dreams across the globe.

It hasn't always been an easy journey or a life of luxury as many believe, but I wouldn't have it any other way. Despite the years of struggle, I succeeded in my one-man mission to make inroads into all these different kinds of cinema, including Hollywood, and cleared the path for others like me to flap their wings and fly out. Today, the world has become a small place, you can go where your heart takes you, but back then, just a passport and visa were not enough to get you work. It took unflagging determination and a never-say-never passion that kept me on course.

Thanks to the global exposure and my experience in international cinema, I was roped in by my dear friend, Pradeep Guha, then a member of the board of directors of the Times of India Group, to judge the Miss India contest for three years. At the time, the Indian perception of beauty was a fair complexion, a sweet, dimpled face and light eyes. My choices were markedly different and opened the eyes of the world to another aspect of Indian beauty. One year it was Diana Hayden who was adjudged Miss World. The next year, Yukta Mookhey sashayed away with the Miss World title. The following year, Lara Dutta and Priyanka Chopra repeated the feat, bagging the Miss Universe and Miss World titles respectively. Then there was Celina Jaitley who also had been my choice. I had coaxed, cajoled and even argued with the other judges at the Miss India contests so that my choices would prevail, knowing the girls were perfect to represent our country at international pageants. I got a crash course from Juhi Chawla, a former Miss India title winner and a friend, as part of my prep on what was appropriate behaviour for a judge, particularly one who was an established onscreen baddie. The girls' victories gave me as much satisfaction and joy as my many blockbusters, and also confirmed Pradeep Guha's far-sightedness and my belief in what would work as Indian beauty for international audiences.

16

SONNY DAYS: SANJAY GROVER

No one consciously chooses to be a single parent. But sometimes circumstances lead you to such a life. It's unfair to assume that the child of a single parent is deprived because every child reacts in a different way. When I became a single parent, my son grew emotionally dependent on me and so did I. Sanjay is the centre of my existence and my emotional being.

My bond with him was cemented the moment he entered the world even though I didn't get to see him on the first two days after his birth, only making it to the hospital late on the third day. He had arrived way ahead of the due date, when I was shooting in Chennai for Shyam and Tulsi Ramsay's 3D film *Saamri*. The film featured Rajan Sippy, Arti Gupta, Asha Sachdev and many others, and I shared the good news with my colleagues, distributed sweets and requested that I be allowed to fly to Mumbai. To my dismay, the producers told me that since they were filming with a special 3D camera only available in Chennai, they needed to finish the shoot over the next two weeks or the film was doomed. They couldn't shoot without me because I was there in every scene and only agreed to let me off on the third day to fly down to Mumbai to see my son for a few hours.

My family was calling constantly, urging me to dash down immediately. I confided in my colleagues on the set, including

Aarti, Asha and Rajan, who reasoned that since it was a happy occasion, I shouldn't bring unhappiness to others through my actions. What they were saying made sense, so I stayed back to complete the shoot, naively believing that my son would never get to know my little secret, not realizing that there were many only too happy to enlighten him. Fortunately, it did not diminish his love and it only enhanced mine.

When Sanjay's mother, my first wife Philomina Lobo, and I decided to separate four years later, we mutually agreed that our son would continue to stay with me, and that she could visit him whenever she wished. Though Philomina had no reservations about the arrangement, to my surprise, the magistrate objected to it, arguing that an infant couldn't stay away from his mother. My wife finally convinced the judge that I would be both mother and father to our little boy and I got custody of Sanjay. After that the two Grover boys went to the airport together to wave goodbye to mummy Philomina. All the way back home, my son wanted to know where mummy had gone, why she wouldn't stop crying, why she had kept hugging him and when she would be back. That day, I learnt the art of spinning stories to shield my son from the harsh realities of life that could break his heart.

In the months that followed, life and my love for my son made me learn everything there was to know about bringing up a baby, from changing his clothes and feeding him to cleaning up after him and giving him a bath. Taking on the sole responsibility of a single parent had been an emotional decision. I quickly realized that as a busy and successful actor I didn't have the luxury of sitting at home with my son. For a few days, I took Sanjay along with me to shoots, but a sweltering set and make-up room—there were no air-conditioned vanity vans at the time—was not the best place for a toddler.

If I was able to bring up my baby against all odds, it is because of God's grace, the help of my parents and siblings, the cooperation of my co-stars, producers and directors. I am also grateful for the large hearts of every lady I met, from airhostess in planes who would bring Sanjay warm milk and my mother and sisters who took turns to come from Delhi to be with him, to the wives of friends and neighbours, my heroines, hairdressers, waitresses and his long-time governess, Mary Khan, who helped in every way they could.

My son wanted me with him every moment and it was difficult to explain to a child that I needed to work. Eventually, we figured out a routine. Sanjay accepted that I had to be out during the day, but I had to return before his bedtime or he refused to sleep. I will forever be indebted to my co-stars who would tell the director to take my close-ups first, so I could rush home early to my child. On outdoor shoots, the task became even more difficult. Back then, there were no cell phones, and in small towns and hill stations few telephones for me to make a trunk call. I would drive for miles on sleet-slicked roads, looking for a phone so I could persuade my son to go to bed with his dadi, promising him that I would slip in beside him sometime during the night. One freezing night when it was snowing, I had to drive down from Manali to Kullu to call Mumbai. No driver was ready to make the trip, so a concerned Ajay Devgn drove the car to ensure I didn't meet with an accident.

Sanjay wasn't an easy child to fool. The minute he opened his eyes, he would ask for me. My mother tried telling him that I had come home during the night but had woken up early and left for the shoot. He responded to her white lie by asking for her dupatta. He then went around the house, borrowing the dupattas of all the ladies, and bringing them to his grandmother, he told her that he would use them to tie me up when I returned home that night so that I couldn't run away early the next morning.

I can laugh about all this now, but at that time, I tried not to leave Sanjay alone, even if it meant skipping film parties and premieres. In later years, his emotional dependency also got me into many awkward situations. As he grew up, we had separate bedrooms in our duplex apartment. Sanjay slept with my father, but there were times, when in the middle of the night, he would silently slip out of his bed and, dragging his favourite quilt behind him, steal into my room which was downstairs. Sometimes I would have a lady friend visiting and staying back if it got late. I would have to hurry her into the washroom till my mother arrived. After much coaxing, she would take my son back to his room. Sometimes Sanjay would insist on sleeping with me in my bed. I would pretend to go off to sleep quickly, and after he nodded off, my lady friend would quietly tiptoe out of the house. You usually see such things happening onscreen and laugh over them, but when they happened to me for real, my social life was shot to pieces.

After some time, I was advised to send my son off to a boarding school much against my wishes. He was miserable there, as was I. So, I brought him back home and he stayed with me till he completed his high school in Mumbai. After that, Sanjay decided to go abroad for further studies. I had made a name for myself in Hollywood by then and had friends like Raj and Kumkum Dutt, Ash Gupta and others who were like my extended family in LA. I cajoled him to apply to UCLA while simultaneously doing a yoga teachers' training course. A week before he graduated from the Los Angeles Film School with a degree in Business of Hollywood and Business of Entertainment, a chance encounter with the former chairperson of MGM's Motion Pictures Worldwide and co-CEO, the magnanimous Mary Parent, landed him a plum job at the studio.

Sanjay has always spoken his mind. He was once invited by the CFO of the studio, my dear friend Bedi Singh, to a social event where he dared to criticize a film that Mary Parent had produced. Instead of getting upset, she appreciated his refreshing, out-of-the-box take on cinema and believed he could help her take their films to newer horizons. In June 2009, Sanjay, fresh out of the university, was taken on as 'director, special projects'. It was the first time that any Bollywood kid or a young Indian had been hired as a top executive in a Hollywood studio

He was given an office at the studio's LA headquarters, on the executive floor which housed the chairperson, the CEO, the CFO and various presidents. I will remain eternally grateful to Mary Parent and Bedi Singh for mentoring my son and giving him this opportunity.

Sanjay was soon brushing shoulders with the president, studio director, CEOs, CFOs and other top executives, as also big Hollywood stars like Tom Cruise, who sits on the board of UA which works closely with MGM. He was associated with big projects like *The Zookeeper*, *The Hobbit* series, *Creed* and the James Bond franchise. He continued with my legacy of introducing Hollywood bigwigs to our mainstream Hindi cinema. Mary Parent would say, 'Sanjay was born in Bollywood and raised in Hollywood.'

During my monthly trips to LA, every time I stepped into the MGM Studio lobby where all the Oscar statuettes were displayed, a hundred yards from Sanjay's office, I was the proudest father in the world. I always went with my camera and forced him to pose for me in his office, against the studio's film memorabilia, on the grounds, and with every executive, including presidents and the chairperson, till finally an exasperated Sanjay would protest, saying, 'Dad, I work here! Why are you behaving like a gawky villager in a big city, a kid in Disneyland or an overwhelmed parent when you are a popular star?' After that, he banned me from carrying a camera into the studio.

For many years, my son has been the toast of Hollywood. Being a high-ranking Hollywood executive, a yoga teacher and a favourite of the top bosses, Sanjay could speak his mind and expose them to Bollywood content. Anything I read, saw or learnt, I shared with him, and even as I bombarded him with information, Sanjay would laugh, 'Papa, you have become Gyan TV.'

After fourteen years of being away from my son, I started missing him intensely. Eventually, Sanjay gave in to my constant emotional blackmail and arrived in Mumbai to make movies here. He has grown up with Tiger Shroff, Shraddha Kapoor, Siddhant Kapoor, Sonam Kapoor, Sooraj Pancholi and Athiya Shetty. Tiger and he attended the same American School of Bombay. When Hollywood producer Lawrence Kasanoff shared the script of his next action-thriller with him, Sanjay suggested they bring on board a fresh new face. He recommended his childhood buddy who is known for his martial arts skills, enviable physique and large fan following, especially among youngsters. After a year of discussions, the producer and studio head flew into India in September 2018 to meet Tiger in Mumbai. Due to Sanjay's perseverance and Larry's faith in Sanjay and Tiger, the project has worked out. Larry has signed on Tiger Shroff to play the lead in one of the biggest forthcoming action films—a dream break in Hollywood for a Bollywood star. Sanjay is the co-producer of this film titled *Raptor*.

Bringing his experiences in production, distribution and film financing into Indian cinema, Sanjay plans to produce interesting films at home. When you embark on a new journey, it is difficult to find friends who not only have faith in your vision but also support it in every conceivable way to become a part of the journey. My son has found a supportive partner in Ajay Sethi who ranks amongst the fifty wealthiest Indians in UAE. Ajay is collaborating on five films with Sanjay. He is friends with everyone in Bollywood and connects well with Sanjay and his off-beat ideas. Their first project together is a wedding film which will go on the floors soon.

My son has found another business partner in Shrikant Bhasi, chairman of the Carnival Group. A chance meeting at the IIFA in Tampa, USA, and further interactions with him, made me realize my friend has great vision, far-sightedness and the courage to overcome all odds. Today, Sanjay and Shrikant's Carnival Group are in the process of producing films together.

Another film-maker who has joined hands with my son is Umesh Shukla, an old actor colleague turned writer–director, who has made amazing films like *OMG: Oh My God* and *102 Not Out*. Not surprisingly for someone who made *102 Not Out*, a film revolving around a father and son, Umesh understands the depth of my relationship with my son.

I was at the Lokmat Maharashtrian of the Year Awards, seated next to the chief minister, when this really nice gentleman introduced himself and started talking to me about my work and achievements in Hollywood. That's how I met Mahaveer Jain, producer, distributor and one of Bollywood's biggest influencers. He is an achiever in multiple areas and is always ready to offer advice and assistance. We continued to interact on a number of fronts and Mahaveer bhai is also collaborating on multiple projects with Sanjay who is now recognized as Hollywood's man in India, someone who will locate and highlight talent from our Gen-X stars, those who would be perfect for cross-continental stories. Interest in Indian cinema and its versatile talent has grown considerably since I crossed over. This is the right time for him to build a bridge between the two film industries, a job I started decades ago.

I also have a dream of seeing my son onscreen someday, but not as another 'Bad Man'. Sanjay can play a leading man with rough edges and a streak of darkness, but I wouldn't want him to follow in my footsteps into the don's den or the gangster's lair. He was offered a couple of films earlier, among them the George Clooney-starrer *Syriana*. At that time, I thought he was a little too young to be handling the dual responsibilities of production and acting. I didn't want him to get distracted from what he was doing, and I still believe I was right in discouraging him from facing the camera back then. But today, if he were to get an interesting offer, I would be the first to push him towards it.

I was a happy man when my son started carving out a niche for himself in Hollywood. I am a happier man today to see him make an excellent beginning in Bollywood, the same industry which has given me money, fame and a 'bad' name. After fourteen years, I can once again hear Sanjay's voice in my duplex apartment in Mumbai. It doesn't matter if he isn't always conversing with me. He could be talking to family, friends, or work mates in another room or even on another floor, but just the sound of his voice makes me emotionally satiated. It wasn't easy bringing up my son alone, but if you turned back the clock and left me at the crossroads again, I would take the same decisions. Sometimes, it is best to listen to your heart.

17

YESTERDAY, TODAY, TOMORROW

A few years ago, when I was in Delhi, I passed by my old neighbourhood when a little boy caught my eye. I asked my chauffeur to stop the car and trailed the boy through the narrow gallis to the old theatre where I had once stealthily watched films with my friends as a young boy. As I observed the child from a distance, I saw him put an eye through the hole cut into one of the tin walls and, suddenly, I was flooded with memories.

I inched closer, curious to know what he was watching. As my shoulder nudged his, he looked up at me, startled, and then, with a muffled shriek, he took to his heels. Surprised by his reaction, I went down on my haunches and looked through the hole to see Kesariya Vilayati in action onscreen. Just then, a hand grabbed my collar and hauled me up. I was face to face with a burly watchman whose lathi reminded me of the many beatings I'd once received and whose worn slippers brought back the flip-flop sound of being chased down the dusty tracks.

Even as I was taking his measure, the security guard's baleful eyes suddenly lit up with a flicker of recognition. 'Aren't you . . .?' he started, and I completed the sentence for him with a laugh, 'Bad Man? I am, yes.'

The hand dropped, and the dark frown turned into a welcoming smile. He whipped out a cell phone from his pocket and asked, suddenly hesitant, '*Ek selfie ho jaaye?*' I replied with a smile of my own, '*Ho jaaye,*' and beckoned him to come closer. I noticed the blanket on his shoulder and before I could articulate my surprise, he nodded, 'Yes, it's the same one you have in *Ram Lakhan. Bahut khojne ke baad* I got one exactly like yours.'

I was moved beyond words.

He walked me back to my car and I waved goodbye. As the car picked up speed and took me away from my old world, I wondered what I had done to deserve a place among the celluloid stars. I had been just another common man, like everyone else, changing buses, walking in the rain, desperately holding my bag over my head and breaking into a run, only to reach home wet and bedraggled. I had been like that man standing by the thela, counting a pile of coins and wet notes, waiting to buy the leftover vegetables at the end of the day because they are cheaper. For someone like me to make it big in Bollywood and world cinema was nothing short of a miracle.

I owe it to my parents' blessings. Pitaji and Chaiji visited every place of worship for years to pray for my success. I owe it to my sisters. They kept fasts religiously and even gave up their savings to finance my stay in Mumbai. I owe it to my elder brother, Ramesh bhai, who quit his studies and started working so I wouldn't be called back from Mumbai. I owe it to the ladies in the gurudwaras, to the postman who conscientiously delivered my letters, to my neighbours who consoled my weeping mother when I left for Mumbai, in fact, to my entire locality who went in truckloads to watch my films when I was just starting out.

Looking out of the car window, I suddenly recognized some familiar landmarks. We were passing Punjabi Bagh and I remembered the ladies in the big kothis there who would buy their household supplies from me every week. I remain eternally grateful to the Almighty for bringing these fairy godmothers into my life. They ensured that I didn't have to quit my studies. And

I not only passed high school but also graduated from one of Delhi's premier colleges with distinction.

Every person I have met in my life's journey—from Sunil Dutt saab to Yash Chopra-ji, Surinder Kapoor-uncle to Professor Roshan Taneja, K.C. Bokadia-ji, Pahlaj Nihalani-ji, Romu and Raj Sippy and Shabana Azmi-ji—has always gone out of their way to help me. It's because of their large-heartedness, their teachings and a little bit of luck that, despite not looking like a conventional six-foot baddie, I went on to become one of the top villains in Bollywood. I would like to take this opportunity to also thank all those who defined the art of villainy in Hindi cinema, who were like gurus to me—legendary actors like Pran saab, Prem Chopra saab, Amrish Puri-ji, Kader Khan saab and many others—who not only inspired me but also guided me and helped me evolve in my journey to becoming the 'Bad Man'. Then, not content to remain within my comfort zone, I spread my wings and flew off across the Atlantic. I wanted to push the envelope and at the same time bring my film industry and fraternity the recognition that was long overdue. Today, when I look back, it seems incredible that I embarked on this mission impossible with just a showreel that had me brandishing a gun and only mouthing abuses.

For me, the sky has always been the limit. After making inroads into Hollywood, I ventured into world cinema, making British, French, German, Italian, Malaysian, Canadian, Iranian and Polish movies at a time when people were completely in the dark about their existence. Of course, this meant that life has been a constant struggle as I had to start from scratch, time and time again. But today, I have the satisfaction of having made the transition from Bollywood to Hollywood and bridging the gap between 'our' cinema and world cinema. There were many highs along the way, including the best actor award I received at the New York International Film Festival for my performance as Dada Bhagwan, a spiritual leader, in *Desperate Endeavors*, and being honoured by the BBC for my contribution to global cinema.

I remember with fondness my many meetings with the great Al Pacino who once invited me to watch his play, *Salome*, Oscar Wilde's dramatized version of the Biblical story of King Herod and his stepdaughter Salome. I spent time with Al Pacino backstage as a friend after the performance. What a fanboy moment that was!

Talking of this Hollywood great reminds me of my friend Gautam Singhania and his lovely wife Nawaz whom I have known for a long time. Nawaz is a talented artist and I remember at one of her exhibition-cum-auctions, I had gone and stood next to a portrait of Al Pacino during the bidding. Immediately, the price of the painting went up, and it went on to fetch the highest price that evening. This led the chairman and managing director of the Raymond Group to joke that I was the desi Al Pacino. Our respect and warmth for each other keeps this friendship strong and may bring us together in the future.

Had it not been for my diffidence, I might have even got to dance with a modern-day Salome when I went with yoga guru Bikram Choudhury and his wife Rajashree bhabhi to a gala hosted by Sharon Stone's charity, Planet-Hope, in LA, to raise money for HIV-positive people. Shirley MacLaine, the Oscar-winning actress of *Terms of Endearment*, and Raquel Welch, whom I had met earlier at Rajashree bhabhi's yoga school, were also there. Midway through the charity ball, a dance with the *Basic Instinct* actress was auctioned. The bid started with a few hundred dollars, going up to thousands in seconds. As the figure was raised, Bikram dada kept nudging me towards the dance floor, muttering, 'Go, go, go!' I dragged my feet because I wasn't carrying so much money on me, little realizing that he would have happily lent it to me to live out another fanboy moment. Before I could muster up the courage to raise my hand, someone else beat me to partner Miss Stone. Ah well, not all dreams come true!

At least I can boast of having smoked a cigar with Arnold Schwarzenegger, not just once but thrice. The first time was at his LA restaurant, Swatzi. I had accompanied Madhu Kapoor there during my years of struggle and we got chatting over Arnold's bodybuilding photographs that were up on the walls. He boosted my confidence, insisting that in this cauldron called Hollywood, your name, background, or even the country of your birth is of little importance in your quest for stardom. If you can impress the audience with your skills, there is a place for you in this world of glitz and glamour. On that note, we had smoked a cigar each, he like a connoisseur and me like the novice that I was.

Miraculously, I got a second chance to showcase my smoking skills which I had learnt on camera, when I accompanied casting directors Janet Hirshenson and Jane Jenkins of the James Bond film *Casino Royale*, for which I had been finalized as the villain, to a club in Beverley Hills whose top floor was reserved for Hollywood A-listers, many of whom were cigar connoisseurs. They rented out humidors at such elite clubs to keep their smokes fresh. This time I did better, although Arnold was still miles ahead.

On our third meeting, I discovered Arnold, the playboy, flirting delightedly with his then wife Maria Shriver, wondering who the pretty woman was and why she wouldn't leave him alone. Even 'Terminators' have a heart and a wonderful sense of humour!

Talking about Arnold reminds me of another Hollywood actor and film-maker who is famous for action films like *Bloodsport*, *Double Impact*, the *Kickboxer* franchise and *The Expendables 2*. Along with my dear friend Ashok Amritraj, producer Bhuvan Lall and Viacom Group CEO, Sudhanshu Vats, I'd accompanied Jean-Claude Van Damme to the Belgium Consulate in Delhi. Every one of his countrymen, who was posted in India and held a high position, was at the consulate that evening. Van Damme was given a hero's welcome. The ambassador in his speech referred to him as the country's 'national treasure', which left him teary-eyed.

The next day, at the launch of Ashok Amritraj's autobiography, *Advantage Hollywood,* where Van Damme represented Hollywood while I represented Bollywood, I relived the emotional evening for those who hadn't been there.

For an artiste there is nothing more satisfying than his work being appreciated and applauded. And while the critics took time to warm up to me, my fans love me, and the film fraternity has always been most encouraging. After watching the first print of Shashi Ranjan's *Siyasat,* an impressed Shatrughan Sinha-ji sent me a handwritten letter, delivered at around six in the morning. The words will remain etched in my memory forever: 'After seeing your work, passion and dedication, if I could will my villainy to anyone, it would be you.'

Does this mean the journey has ended for me? No way! Since I have lived a large part of my life in Mumbai's show business, I see myself as a star in the galaxy of light. Sometimes, on a particular dark night, I may not be visible. But the next day, I am back, twinkling brightly in the sky. As an actor, I am still seeking out new roles and boldly going forward.

Mahesh Bhatt saab, Sanjay Dutt and I have reunited for a sequel to *Sadak,* which also marks Bhatt saab's comeback as a director after two decades. I play the 'Bad Man' in *Sadak 2* which I am sure will bring the menacing khalnayak back. The film also features Aditya Roy Kapur and Alia Bhatt whom I saw grow up before my eyes. It reunites Sanjay and Pooja Bhatt, the leads of *Sadak,* after twenty-eight years. It's a new journey for my brother Sanju and me too. We started out together with *Rocky,* almost four decades ago, and have made thirty films along the way.

Then, there is Rohit Shetty's *Sooryavanshi* with Akshay Kumar and Katrina Kaif. It's one of the lead roles that is impossible to bracket as either the hero or the villain because my character's sense of what is good and bad is blurred. The first thing that struck me when I entered Rohit's cop universe was his dedication and passion for cinema. He is driven by work and obsessed with the film he is making.

My zest, excitement and energy remain undimmed, but there are times when I feel a little lost in this new world in which my son thrives today. Once I had taken him by his hand and taught him how to walk. Today, Sanjay is the one holding out his hand to me. I reach out to take it, knowing it's too early to rest on my laurels. I will continue to live for today with the hope of a brighter tomorrow for my son.

Like every parent, individual achievements fade away in the face of your child's success. Once, my parents had hoped, prayed and waited anxiously to see my name light up the marquee. Today, the dream is to see another name light up the marquee—that of Sanjay Grover.

INDEX